Do Not Forget Me

War and Genocide

General Editors: Omer Bartov, Brown University; A. Dirk Moses, University of Sydney

In recent years there has been a growing interest in the study of war and genocide, not from a traditional military history perspective, but within the framework of social and cultural history. This series offers a forum for scholarly works that reflect these new approaches.

The Berghahn series Studies on War and Genocide *has immeasurably enriched the English-language scholarship available to scholars and students of genocide and, in particular, the Holocaust.*—**Totalitarian Movements and Political Religions**

Recent volumes:

Volume 32
Do Not Forget Me: Three Jewish Mothers Write to Their Sons from the Thessaloniki Ghetto
Edited by Leon Saltiel

Volume 31
The Herero Genocide: War, Emotion, and Extreme Violence in Colonial Namibia
Matthias Häussler

Volume 30
Voices on War and Genocide: Three Accounts of the World Wars in a Galician Town
Edited and with an Introduction by Omer Bartov

Volume 29
A Sad Fiasco: Colonial Concentration Camps in Southern Africa, 1900–1908
Jonas Kreienbaum

Volume 28
The Holocaust in Bohemia and Moravia: Czech Initiatives, German Policies, Jewish Responses
Wolf Gruner

Volume 27
Probing the Limits of Categorization: The Bystander in Holocaust History
Edited by Christina Morina and Krijn Thijs

Volume 26
Let Them Not Return: Sayfo—The Genocide against the Assyrian, Syriac, and Chaldean Christians in the Ottoman Empire
Edited by David Gaunt, Naures Atto, and Soner O. Barthoma

Volume 25
Daily Life in the Abyss: Genocide Diaries, 1915–1918
Vahé Tachjian

Volume 24
Microhistories of the Holocaust
Edited by Claire Zalc and Tal Bruttmann

Volume 23
The Making of the Greek Genocide: Contested Memories of the Ottoman Greek Catastrophe
Erik Sjöberg

For a full volume listing, please see the series page on our website:
http://berghahnbooks.com/series/war-and-genocide

Do Not Forget Me

Three Jewish Mothers Write to Their Sons from the Thessaloniki Ghetto

Edited by
Leon Saltiel

With Forewords by Serge Klarsfeld and Yannis Boutaris

Letters translated from French by Jenny Demetriou

berghahn
NEW YORK • OXFORD
www.berghahnbooks.com

First published in 2021 by
Berghahn Books
www.berghahnbooks.com

English-language edition

First paperback edition published 2024

Greek-language edition

Originally published in Greek by Alexandria as
"Mi me xehasete"

Library of Congress Cataloging-in-Publication Data

A C.I.P. cataloging record is available from the Library of Congress
Library of Congress Cataloging in Publication Control Number: 2021935801

British Library Cataloguing in Publication Data

A catalogue record for this book is available from the British Library.

ISBN 978–1-80073-105-9 hardback
ISBN 978-1-80539-134-0 paperback
ISBN 978-1-80539-411-2 epub
ISBN 978–1-80073-107-3 web pdf

https://doi.org/10.3167/9781800731059

Contents

List of Illustrations vii

Foreword to the English Edition ix
Serge Klarsfeld

Foreword to the Greek Edition xi
Yannis Boutaris

Acknowledgments xii

Introductory Note from the Jewish Museum of Greece xvi
Zanet Battinou

Timeline of Anti-Jewish Measures in Nazi-Occupied Thessaloniki xviii

Maps xxi

Translation Note xxiii
Leon Saltiel and Jenny Demetriou

Introduction: Historical Context xxv
Leon Saltiel

Prologue: Instructions to Jews Migrating from Thessaloniki xlix

List of Letters li

Part I. Saltiel Letters

Introduction 3
Eleni Saltiel

Short Biography of Maurice Saltiel 11
Eleni Saltiel

Excerpts from the Autobiography of Maurice Saltiel 13

Letters from Sarina (Sara) Saltiel 17

Part II. Barouh Letters

Introduction 57
Leon Saltiel

Letters from Mathilde Barouh 63

Part III. Cazes Letters

Introduction 77
Leon Saltiel

Letters from Neama Cazes 85

Bibliography 109

Illustrations

Maps

0.1. Triple Occupation of Greece by the Axis Powers (1941–44). xxi

0.2. Occupied Thessaloniki, 1943, with the Jewish ghettos and other points of interest. xxii

Figures

0.1. An envelope sent to Neama Cazes on 13 April 1943, which was returned to sender as the recipient had "departed from Thessaloniki." Italian censorship tape and stamps are visible. xxviii

0.2. Jewish men of Thessaloniki gathered in Liberty Square and forced to undergo humiliating gymnastics to register for forced labor. German soldiers stand in the back and watch. xxxi

0.3. A group of friends wearing the yellow star in the ghetto of Thessaloniki, March–April 1943. The second woman from the left is Alice Bivas, who perished at Auschwitz together with her parents. She sent this photograph to her family. xxxii

0.4. Transport of Jews from the ghetto in the eastern part of Thessaloniki to the Baron Hirsch transit camp, via Egnatia Street, 9 April 1943. The Jews can be seen in between two columns of onlookers who are watching the scene. The photo was taken from a balcony, where one can also see the father and sister of the photographer. xxxiv

1.1. Sarina Serrero Saltiel. 4

1.2. Isaak, Sarina, and Maurice Saltiel, at a young age, in the spa town of Karlsbad. 5

1.3. Isaak and Sarina Saltiel with little Maurice. 7

1.4. From left: Sotiris Faltsis, Giannis Triantafyllidis, and Maurice Saltiel, standing, during a school holiday of the Second Boys High School of Thessaloniki. 9

1.5. Maurice and Sarina Saltiel. 14

1.6. The first page of Sarina Saltiel's letter of 17 March 1943. 16

2.1. Mathilde Barouh in her wedding dress. 58

2.2. Fredy Barouh in the British Royal Air Force Regiment, September 1944 to June 1945. 59

2.3. Mathilde Barouh and her children, Lily and Fredy. 60

2.4. The first page of Mathilde Barouh's letter of 13 April 1943. 61

3.1. Neama Cazes. 78

3.2. Neama and Juda Cazes. 80

3.3. Certificate of Service of the General Headquarters of the Middle East Forces, to Maurice (Anthony) Cazes for his contribution "to the liberation of Europe," 14 February 1945. 82

3.4. Top row, from left to right: Nektarios and Matilda Chrysochoou, Albertos and Ioanna Cazes, Matilda's parents. Second row: Fani Cazes, Jo Nahmias and his daughter, Renee, from Paris, and Maurice Cazes. Photograph from the wedding of Matilda Cazes with Nektarios Chrysochoou, 1975. 83

3.5. The first page of Neama Cazes's letter of 5 March 1943. 84

Foreword to the English Edition

As time goes by, the suffering of victims gives way to the fascination their executioners hold. The twentieth century will be representative of Hitler just as the seventeenth century is representative of Genghis Khan. It is difficult to find an editor for touching letters written by Jewish mothers who perished in Auschwitz. On the other hand, if insignificant letters from Eva Braun to her beloved Adolf were to be discovered, they would immediately be published worldwide. These letters from Sarina, Mathilde, and Neama to their sons symbolize modesty, sincerity, dignity, maternal love, anguish and devotion for family and friends, courage in the face of adversity, the prospect of a cruel death for themselves and probably for all their loved ones, nostalgia for their past lives, and the annihilation of Jewish Salonica and everything they loved. These letters represent civilization and humanity, as we understand them today, in the face of Nazi barbarism allied with the ferocious greed of the local population. They are a reflection of a peaceful, hardworking, and emotional people who were incapable of conceiving the absolute evil that emanated from the horde of swastika-clad demons who had taken possession of them, and who were helpless in the face of the relentless anti-Jewish hatred—a hatred that eradicated them from the face of the earth after centuries of existence and positive influence.

These letters deeply move us, not only because we know what happened after the last letters were sent but also because they make us fear an uncertain future, as our mothers, wives, and daughters have much in common with these Jewish women who were tortured slowly for months in Salonica before being gassed and burned in Auschwitz in the spring of 1943. One must absolutely read these letters from the point of view of a mother, not from a historical perspective, in order to be informed of what happened during the Holocaust and for us to decide what our commitment should be so that we do not to find ourselves in the same situation.

Serge Klarsfeld
June 2020

Foreword to the Greek Edition

We all know, some of us better than others, through postwar testimonies what happened during the period of the anti-Jewish persecution. However, this collection, thanks to its rich content and the time span it covers, constitutes an invaluable historic artifact—testimony of the horrible reality endured by fifty thousand fellow Jewish Thessalonian citizens.

It consists of fifty-three letters written by three Jewish mothers, who narrate their everyday life in the ghetto, away from their children, a life that with each coming day leads closer and closer to death. Through the pages of this book, the sacred relationship between mother and child is highlighted, which nothing can reverse, not even the inhuman Nazi regime.

The tragedy of the events and the detail of the description deeply move the reader, as the narration pertains to simple citizens, individuals with education, high ideals, industriousness, and love for their family and their city. These citizens, whom the authoritarian formation of Nazism wanted to annihilate, are part of this death toll our homeland in general and Thessaloniki in particular was forced to pay, losing a part of its own self, that of its Jewish inhabitants.

Yiannis Boutaris
Mayor of Thessaloniki 2011–19

Acknowledgments

In the course of my PhD research at the University of Macedonia in Thessaloniki—which has since been published[1]—I was particularly interested in finding contemporary sources on the Holocaust in Thessaloniki. The sources I have found record the events as they happen, and thus are free from hindsight, very valuable in determining knowledge and emotions of the particular period and evaluating any reactions, or lack thereof, that may have followed, in their own context.

I first learned about the letters of Neama Cazes from Mark Mazower's book, *Salonica: City of Ghosts*.[2] There, Mazower cited an excerpt published by Nikos Stavroulakis in the newsletter of the Jewish Museum of Greece.[3] Later, when I curated the exhibition *Salonique, épicentre de la destruction des Juifs de Grèce* [Thessaloniki, epicenter of the destruction of the Jews of Greece] at the Memorial de la Shoah in Paris, 1 December 2013 to 16 March 2014, the Jewish Museum of Greece in Athens and the Jewish Museum of Thessaloniki contributed copies of letters by Mathilde Barouh and Sara Saltiel respectively.

I wish to thank the Jewish Museum of Greece, in particular its director Zanet Battinou, and Eleni Saltiel for providing me with copies and the permission to publish the three full collections of letters, as well as Anastasia Loudarou, Christina Meri, and Erika Perahia for their assistance.

Since the publication of this book in Greek, more letters have come to my attention and have been included in the English edition. Daniele Covo, Mathilde Barouh's granddaughter, gave me copies of a letter sent to her family in Argentina, which included a letter from her grandmother. Unfortunately, Daniele passed away in April 2020 and could not see this publication, which she so much supported. Marie Cazes, Neama Cazes's little niece, gave me additional letters exchanged between Ms. Cazes and her sons, copies that were given to her father Albert by her uncle Maurice Cazes.

I owe special thanks to Renate Modiano for her invaluable help in reading and transcribing the letters. Her knowledge of languages, her patience, and the fact that she grew up with the authors' generation helped decipher many words that seemed incomprehensible in the manuscripts.

Eleni Saltiel showed great willingness and care with the publication of the letters from her mother-in-law. She provided the introductory texts and prepared their translation for the Greek volume. The current English volume includes an additional biographical note of her late husband, Maurice Saltiel.

Morris Barouh and Daniele Covo, grandchildren of Mathilde Barouh, provided me with important biographical information. Morris Barouh also gave me information on his father Fredy. Similarly, Irini Hadjimihail, Matilda Chrysochoou, and Marie Cazes gave me important information on Neama Cazes, her two sons, and her family.

I would like to thank Aliki Arouh, responsible for the Historical Archive of the Jewish Community of Thessaloniki, for her valuable help in identifying not only Neama but also many other people who appear in the letters. She thus gave a name and a voice to other people, the overwhelming majority of whom were victims of the Holocaust.

I had the unique opportunity to visit Sotiris Faltsis, one of the people appearing in the letters, in his apartment in Thessaloniki in July 2015. Mr. Faltsis gave me very useful information about his family and other people who appeared in the letters, even though he could not recall other names or events after so many years. Unfortunately, Mr. Faltsis passed away a few months later, and we could not seek any more clarifications.

A first article with excerpts of the letters was published in a special volume of the *Journal of Southeast European and Black Sea Studies*,[4] and then republished in book format some months later.[5] I would like to thank the journal's editor, Ioannis Armakolas, for the invitation to contribute my own research, and also the editors of the special volume—Giorgos Antoniou, Katerina Kralova, and Marija Vulesica—whose many important comments have been integrated in the introduction of the present volume.

I would like to thank Alexandria Publications, its director Takis Fragoulis, the series editor Giorgos Antoniou, and Vicky Lekka and Evropi Koutsogianni for enthusiastically accepting my proposal to publish the collection of the letters from the three mothers in Greek.[6] Their help with the preparation of the manuscript, its publication, and its subsequent promotion was invaluable. We organized two book presentations, in Athens and in Thessaloniki, and we were honored to have a full room at both events. The Athens presentation, in June 2018, featured opening remarks by Zanet Battinou, and the presenters were Stavros Zouboulakis, president of the Supervisory Council of the National Library of Greece; Efstathios Lianos-Liantis, the special secretary for religious and cultural diplomacy of the Greek Foreign Ministry; and Anna Fragoudaki, professor emeritus of the University of Athens. The presentation was moderated by journalist Nikos Vatopoulos. Actress Margarita Papagianni read excerpts of the letters. In Thessaloniki, the event took place in the "Maurice Saltiel Hall" of the Thessaloniki Concert Hall, named after one of the sons who received the correspondence. The event, in January 2019, featured opening remarks by Yannis Boutaris, mayor of Thessaloniki and David Saltiel, president of the Central Council of Greek Jewish Communities and of the Jewish Community of Thessaloniki. Presentations were made by Giorgos Antoniou, Jewish studies chair at the University of Thessaloniki; Nikos Marantzidis, professor of the University of Macedonia; and Sofia Nikolaidou, author. Journalist Sofia Christoforidou moderated the event, and actress Sofia Voulgari read excerpts of letters.

The book had a very positive reception in the country. Book reviews were published in several newspapers, journals, and blogs. I was interviewed on TV and radio. Groups of high school students prepared videos based on the letters, and the book has also been included in university courses. In addition, documentary makers, artists, and cultural events organizers have started to realize works based on, inspired by, or including these letters, and I would like to briefly highlight two such important initiatives. The first took place in October 2020 in the framework of the annual Dimitria festival, the leading cultural institution of Thessaloniki hosted by the city of Thessaloniki. The letters were read in a three-part series, under the art direction of Akis Sakellariou and directed by Grigoris Apostolopoulos, by actresses Roula Pateraki and Efi Stamouli as well as the President of the Greek Republic Katerina Sakellaropoulou, together with traditional Sephardic songs and other essays. The second was a dance-theatre performance by Andromachi Dimitriadou Lindhal and her dance company, Asomates Dynameis, entitled "Is it true that you will always wait for me?" which premiered in Nicosia, Cyprus is November 2020.

With regards to the English translation, I would like to thank Professor Dirk Moses for positively recommending this volume to Berghahn Books, as well as the three anonymous reviewers for their valuable feedback. Mykelin Higham and Chris Chappell were supportive from the beginning and guided me with their feedback and insights through the preparation process.

I would like to express my appreciation to Jenny Demetriou-Saltiel who undertook the translation of the letters from French to English, with a lot of care and attention. I wrote the introductory note as well as two of the three texts introducing the letter series. I would like to thank Serge Klarsfeld for providing the introduction to the English edition, and also Mayor Yannis Boutaris for providing an introduction to the Greek edition, which has been included in the present edition.

I would also like to thank Marie Cazes, Matilda Chrysochou, Daniele Covo, and Eleni and Simo Saltiel for providing me with photos of the three authors and their families for this publication. In addition, thanks to Mario Soustiel for preparing the maps that illustrate this book and Dimitris Mitsopoulos for compiling the index. Finally, I would like to thank my family and friends who have warmly supported this project and encouraged me to continue its dissemination in different languages.

Notes

1. Saltiel, *Holocaust*.
2. Mazower, *Salonica*, 405.
3. Stavroulakis, "Letters."
4. Saltiel, "Voices."
5. Kralova et al., *Jewish Life*, 48–67.
6. Saltiel, *"Mi Me Xehasete."*

Introductory Note from the Jewish Museum of Greece

The collections of the Jewish Museum of Greece (JMG) comprise more than ten thousand original objects and archives, material remains of twenty-three hundred years of Jewish presence in Greece. The museum was founded in 1977 with the purpose of research, collection, study, preservation, publication, and exhibition of these artifacts, which relate to the history, customs, written and oral traditions, and everyday life of Greek Jews.

The core of its collections, apart from the very few objects collected by the Jewish Community of Athens after World War II, was composed of the objects that were returned by the Bulgarian government upon the rise of communism to power. Personal objects, jewelry, household items, synagogue utensils, and documents belonging to the Jews of the cities of Eastern Macedonia and Thrace, confiscated during the period of the Bulgarian occupation and recorded in detail, became the first complete and extended set of the JMG's collection.

Today they comprise the historic and substantive core of the Holocaust Collection. One of the five basic collections of the JMG, the one relevant to the Second World War and the Holocaust, is rich in rare historical documents, archival material, testimonies, newspapers, magazines, photographs, IDs and cloth yellow stars, personal items from the Occupation period, and finally, objects and uniforms from concentration and extermination camps. The category of testimonies includes also the Archive of Oral History, which numbers today some 130 audiovisual interviews, primarily of Greek survivors of the Holocaust both from our country and from their current countries of residency, including Italy, France, the United States, and Israel.

This valuable material allows the museum to offer to the visitor an experiential recording of history, enriched with original, multidimensional objects, documents, photographs, and audiovisual material. The museum experience gives authenticity and substance to the process of discovery and learning, as the combination of the artifacts and the museum narrative highlights the history of the Holocaust through the voice of the historical subject. In addition, it presents a picture of history as a living and evolving narrative with multifaceted issues, a lasting and fascinating subject of study that concerns us all.

In the JMG Holocaust Collection belong the letters from Neama Cazes and Mathilde Barouh from Thessaloniki, which were happily provided and published in this book in memory of members of the local community and all Greek Jews killed in the Nazi camps. Reinforced by the rest of the relevant material identified and studied by the editor Leon Saltiel, they vividly convey to the reader the climate of uncertainty, confusion, anxiety, fear, terror, and panic faced by the Jews of Europe at that time. Through the troubled words of the two women unfolds the anguish of the scattered families, of a community that was decimated, and of a whole world entangled in a dark and frightening adventure of persecution and extermination, from which few voices have emerged to narrate.

Zanet Battinou
Director of the Jewish Museum of Greece
November 2017

Timeline of Anti-Jewish Measures in Nazi-Occupied Thessaloniki

9 April 1941	Entrance of German soldiers to Thessaloniki.
11 April	Closure of Jewish newspapers.
14 May	Final deadline to hand in all radios owned by Jews.
May–November	Special Taskforce Rosenberg plunders the archives of the Jewish Community, synagogues, and libraries.
11 July 1942	Assembly of male Jews in Liberty Square to register for forced labor, public humiliation.
July–October	3,500 Jews used for forced labor around the whole of country under harsh conditions.
17 October	Agreement between Merten and Community to release the workers in exchange for the payment of ransom and the destruction of the Jewish cemetery.
6 December	Beginning of destruction of Jewish cemetery.
13 January 1943	Preparatory visit to Thessaloniki of Adolf Eichmann's envoy, Rolf Günther.
6 February	Arrival of a team of SS and German police to Thessaloniki, headed by Dieter Wisliceny and Alois Brunner—issuing of first antisemitic orders.
11 February	Prohibition of Jews to use the tram and any other means of transportation and to circulate in the street after sunset.

	Census of all Jews except those residing in Jewish neighborhoods.
25 February	Confinement in ghettos, yellow star, signs in Jewish business, prohibition to use the telephone.
	Deletion of Jews from unions, associations, organizations, chambers of commerce, which made impossible the professional employment of a large part of the population.
1 March	Obligation to submit declaration of assets.
4 March	The Baron Hirsch neighborhood, opposite the train station, fenced with boards and barbed wire, residents forbidden to exit.
6 March	Jewish neighborhoods marked with a yellow line.
7 March	Establishment of the Agency for the Custody of Jewish Properties (YDIP), with the goal to register Jewish assets (shops and apartments) and appoint custodians.
15 March	First train to Auschwitz, transporting 2,400 people,[1] residents of Baron Hirsch neighborhood, as well as the 15 Jewish families of the town of Lagadas.
17 March	Second train transporting 2,500 people, residents of Agia Paraksevi and Small Station neighborhoods.
19 March	Third train transporting 2,500 people, residents of Rezi Vardar neighborhood.
23 March	Fourth train transporting 2,800 people. After the evacuation of the northern districts and the urban ghetto, the neighborhoods of Campagne, 6, 151, and Kalamaria follow.
24 March	Arrests in 151 neighborhood and transport of 1,000 men to forced labor camps.
26 March	Decision of Municipality of Thessaloniki to rename streets bearing Jewish names.
27 March	Fifth train transporting 2,800 people.
3 April	Sixth train transporting 2,800 people.
5 April	Seventh train transporting 2,800 people.
7 April	Eighth train transporting 2,800 people.
10 April	Ninth train transporting 2,800 people.

13 April	Tenth train transporting 2,800 people.
16 April	Eleventh train transporting 2,800 people.
20 April	Twelfth train transporting 2,800 people.
22 April	Thirteenth train transporting 2,800 people.
28 April	Fourteenth train transporting 2,600 people.
3 May	Fifteenth train transporting 2,600 people. This convoy also included 660 Jews from Veria and 350 Jews from Florina.
9 May	Sixteenth train destined for Auschwitz, transporting 1,500 people, including the Jews of the Evros region on the border with Turkey, 740 from Didimotiho, 180 from Nea Orestiada, and 30 from Soufli.
1 June	Transport of 820 people to Auschwitz, members of the Community board and staff.
15 July	Train transporting 322 Jews of Italian citizenship to Athens. The same day, a few dozen Jews of other nationalities (Swiss, Turkish, Persian) also left.
2 August	Train destined for Bergen-Belsen, transporting 74 "privileged" Greek Jews and 367 Jews of Spanish citizenship.
10 August	Transport of 1,800 Jews to Auschwitz who were previously employed in forced labor works.

Notes

1. The information on the departures from Greece comes from a letter sent by the Greek Railway Company (SEK) to the Jewish Community of Thessaloniki on 9 January 1945. The SEK called the numbers "rough" and in need of additional checking. On the arrivals at Auschwitz, the source is the records of the Auschwitz Museum as collected by Czech, *Auschwitz*. Czech also speaks of the numbers being estimates. These sources have been published in Fleischer, *Crown and Swastika*, 344, and Handrinos, "Trains." The numbers and dates for the seventeenth and nineteenth convoys come from Molho and Nehama, *In Memoriam*, 120–21.

Maps

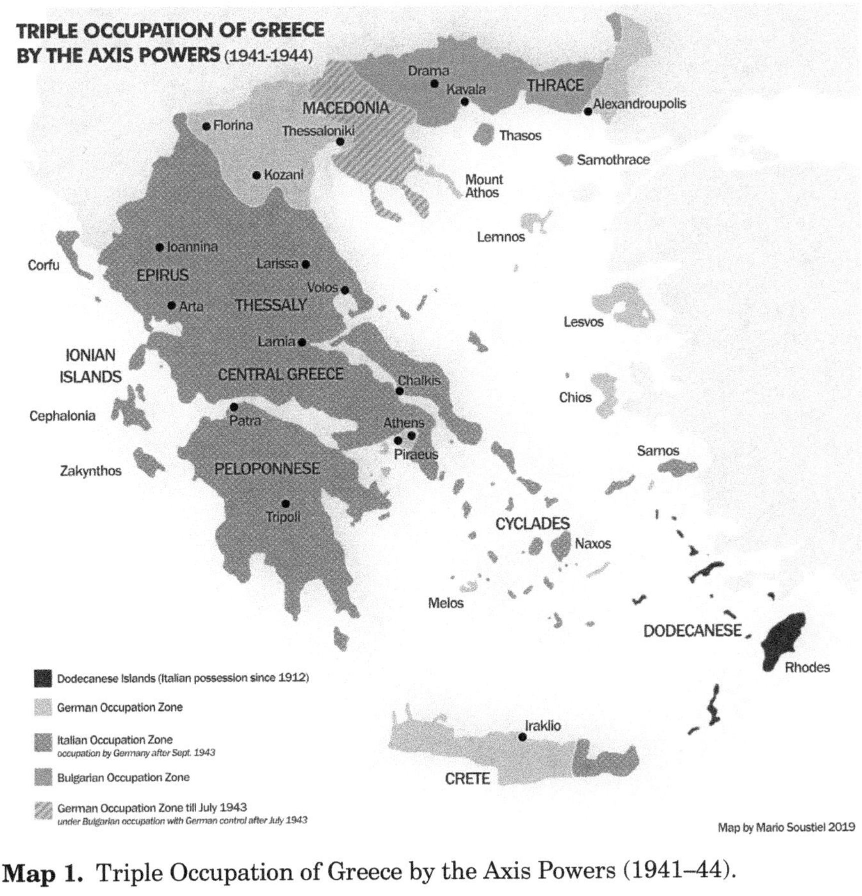

Map 1. Triple Occupation of Greece by the Axis Powers (1941–44).

Map 2. Occupied Thessaloniki, 1943, with the Jewish ghettos and other points of interest.

Translation Note

Leon Saltiel and Jenny Demetriou

One of the first decisions in publishing the English version of the letters from the three mothers was how to transliterate their names. In the Greek edition, we had opted for a phonetic transcription, similar to the way the families spell their names in Greek today. However, certain problems emerged on the choice of the name in a Latin alphabet.The easiest choice concerned Sara Saltiel, as this is the way she spelled her name, which also fits the Greek transliteration. For her son's name, we opted for "Maurice," the way his mother would address the letters to him in French, instead of the more Greek-looking name of "Moris."

For the second mother, we chose the French version of her name as "Mathilde Barouh," which is the name she used in her documents. She addressed her son in the letters as "Fredy."

Finally, for the third mother, we chose "Neama Cazes." This was not an easy choice. In her son's documents, the name appears also as "Cases," "Kases," and "Kazes," the last being the way we usually transliterate the name in Greek. Her family in France today uses the name "Cazès," so we opted for this option minus the accent. For her two sons, we followed the way she would write to them in French, using "Maurice" and "Berto."

For all the other names that appear in the letters, for people, streets, and places, we have kept their spelling as it appeared in the text.

The general comment of the translator was that she tried to keep the authors' style throughout, even though the language was awkward at times, including sentence structure and flow of thoughts. She took some liberty in interpreting certain words/sentences that would otherwise not have made any sense in English. On rare occasions, where sentences made little sense in French or where the original manuscript was illegible or missing, we opted for the closest text that sounded plausible.

As the texts included sentences and phrases in Judeo-Spanish and words in Greek, Turkish, and Hebrew, we chose to translate all of them in English, indicating in an endnote the original choice of language and script. In that way, we tried to preserve some of the multilingualism of the letters, which would otherwise be lost in a translation.

Introduction

Historical Context

Leon Saltiel

Between 15 March and 10 August 1943, some forty-three thousand Jews of Thessaloniki were transported to the Nazi death camp of Auschwitz. Of those, less than one thousand returned back alive. This was a devastating blow to the Jewish population of Thessaloniki, a major Jewish center in Europe since the arrival of the Sephardic Jews after the Spanish Inquisition in 1492. The Jews had constituted the majority of the population—and at times even the absolute majority—thus marking the city's character for centuries.

One of the most comprehensive first attempts to document the Holocaust in Thessaloniki, and in Greece in general, was the book by Michael Molho and Joseph Nehama, *In Memoriam*.[1] Based on their own experiences, survivor testimonies, and the scant documentation that was available at the time, the two authors tried to reconstruct the Nazi period, the antisemitic measures, and the last days of the Jewish communities. This work, whose first volume was written in 1948, was coupled with some of the early survivors' testimonies that were printed mostly privately.[2] Molho also tapped into the diary of Yomtov Yacoel, the Thessaloniki Jewish Community's legal counsel, who played a central role in the events of the period.[3] As his diary is based most probably on detailed notes he kept each day, it remains an authentic and invaluable record of the Nazi persecution in Thessaloniki. Scholarly works that have appeared since have tried to combine these first testimonies together with diplomatic and government archives, newspaper articles, and trial records in an effort to provide a more complete picture.[4]

However, little is known about the everyday lives of individual Jews during the years of the Nazi occupation, let alone the period of ghettoization and deportation. Most of the existing information comes from testimonies of Jewish survivors or Christian neighbors after the war. Very little material is available from eyewitness accounts of the Nazi antisemitic measures during the events, free from hindsight and the influence of what had followed. This gap in historiography can be bridged by a unique find: a series of fifty-three letters written by three Jewish mothers living in Thessaloniki and sent to their sons, all residing in Athens—all three women victims of the Holocaust. This considerable number of letters from three different eyewitnesses, as well as the period covered (which goes until their transfer to the Baron Hirsch ghetto, which served as a transit camp for the deportation by train to Auschwitz-Birkenau), can shed light on the lives of ordinary Jewish citizens of Thessaloniki, never before known in such detail. The collections seem to be almost complete, as no significant gaps in the narration could be found, thus covering the period in question quite consistently.

Letters are an uncommon find as they often remain in the possession of the family, outside the reach of the researcher. In addition, when found, letters can be fragmented, or lacking the information sought by the historian. In this respect, this collection is rather extraordinary, not only because of the great volume, rich content, and near completeness of the series but also because of the fact that they come from three different authors—three mothers who write to their sons—thus adding a rare multiperspectivity within a common pattern.

The three mothers who are the primary authors are Sara Saltiel, Mathilde Barouh and Neama Cazes. Between 17 May 1942 and 21 March 1943, Sara (Sarina) Serrero Saltiel (1902–43) sent twenty-eight letters to her son Maurice, who was located in Athens. Eleven letters from Mathilde Kamhi Barouh (1883–1943) to her son Fredy have survived, sent from 28 February 1943 to 17 April 1943. Neama Djivre Cazes (1889–1943) sent fourteen letters initially to her son Maurice and then to both of her sons, Maurice and Alberto, between 29 January 1943 and 10 April 1943. The largest collection of letters comprises those sent from Sara Saltiel to her son Maurice Saltiel in Athens, which cover approximately ten months. The letters from the mothers make up the largest part of the collection. Within them, additional letters were found, sent by other family members or close friends, which the recipients also kept in their possession and, in this way, have been preserved to this day. These letters have also been included in this volume.

The three women, aged between forty and sixty years old, had sons in their twenties or thirties. They were from middle-class families, although it is hard to ascertain their exact social status, as the war situation seriously affected everyone's lives and well-being. The Saltiel family seems to be the wealthiest of the three, judging from lifestyle and business aspects described in the letters. The other two families had more limited means and could be described as belonging to the lower middle class. They do not seem to have contacts with the leadership or the elders of the Jewish Community, who had assumed important roles during this period. Whatever they write is what they saw, heard, or lived themselves. Moreover, it is almost certain that the three mothers were not in direct contact with one another.

Another interesting element offered by these letters is the female perspective, and that of the mother in particular. Women are often absent from the historical narration, and their role is presented as secondary. Consequently, a significant part of the population is not represented in historiography, and their experiences are marginalized. In this collection, the women have the principle voice, as they are the narrators of the dramatic events of the German occupation. We not only read their voice but also view the events as presented through their own lens. Their role in the Jewish family becomes apparent, and the areas of their prime responsibility are highlighted, such as care for the family and friends, contact with their children, daily housekeeping, and the preparation of the meals. Thus, this special and unique perspective is added to the other valuable information contained in these letters.

Greece during 1942 and 1943 was divided into three occupation zones by Germany and its Italian and Bulgarian allies. More relevant in our case is the border line between the German and Italian zones, as Thessaloniki was under German control and Athens under Italian control (see map 0.1). As the Italians did not wish to implement antisemitic measures in their territories, these became safe havens for Jews, with several hundred fleeing Thessaloniki to go to the southern parts of the country, most of them to Athens.[5] These included the four sons, who were already located there or moved soon after the Nazis started to implement racial laws in Thessaloniki.

The letters were sent from Thessaloniki either by regular post or through different Greek Christian acquaintances who made the journey to Athens and could circulate rather freely between these two zones. The confinement of the Jews to the ghettos did not prohibit the postman from accessing the recipients and delivering correspondence addressed to them. The letters took around four to five days to arrive, though not all letters made it.

It is important to note that there appear to be no marks on the letters indicating any state censorship, even though the letters were sent and received by Jews, including during the period of the deportations. The three mothers mentioned that some of the letters, either theirs or those of their sons, did not reach their destination. This could be due to the bad postal system and the difficulties during the war. Since the publication of the Greek volume, some additional letters have come to our attention, including letters written by Neama Cazes's sons in April 1943 and returned back to them in Athens. The envelope bears stamps as well as a sticker by Italian censorship. Additionally, a handwritten note in Greek states, "Departed from Thessaloniki."[6] Similar stamps can be seen in the letter of Mathilde Barouh sent to her daughter in Paris in June 1943.

Occasionally, the mothers could speak with their sons over the phone, but with difficulties in the connection. For example, on 24 January 1943, Sara Saltiel had started speaking with her son on the phone when the line was cut. Fredy Barouh was able to call friends in Thessaloniki until at least the beginning of April. The mothers had to go to a friend or relative who had a phone connection, usually in their office, and wait for hours for the call.[7]

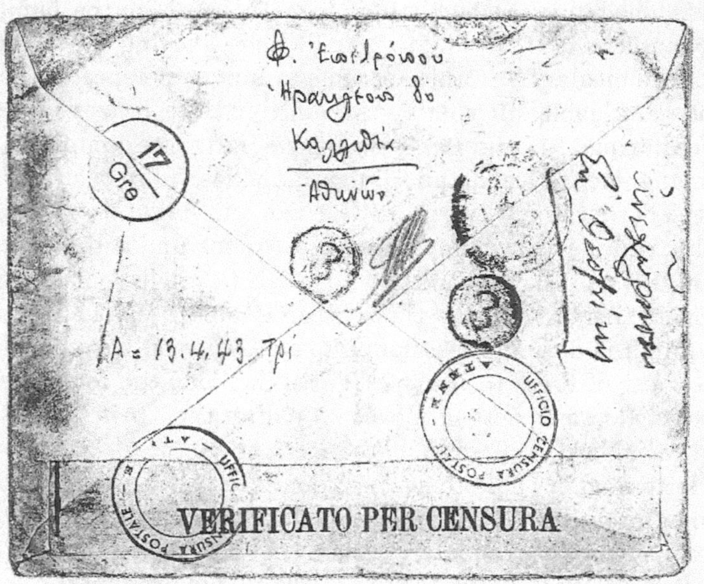

Figure 0.1. An envelope sent to Neama Cazes on 13 April 1943, which was returned to sender as the recipient had "departed from Thessaloniki." Italian censorship tape and stamps are visible. Archive of Marie Cazes.

These pages of testimony by the three mothers bear a lot of similarities. The letters are very charged emotionally. The authors described their feelings, fears, prayers, and anguish, which escalated as they realized that their final days were approaching. The correspondence between mother and son is, at times, deeply touching and moving, and radiates an extraordinary humanity. The mothers could not hide the great love they felt for their sons and provided them with last words of advice.

Moreover, the letters detail aspects of daily life, which was quite challenging because of the war situation and eventually the antisemitic restrictions. Spending their time each day was a challenge, as the Jews were confined in the ghettos, without work or any particular activities. They had to depend on family, friends, and neighbors. It is important to stress that these letters offer the fullest and most comprehensive description of the daily life in the ghetto and the emotions right before and during the deportations in Thessaloniki that have been discovered so far.

Each of the three mothers had their own social circles, family and friends, business partners, and neighbors. Consequentially, through their letters, the reader is able to find information about several dozens of other people who interact with the main narrators.

Even if the mothers may have censored themselves—not to describe fully the situation and disturb their sons—they did pass on private discussions, gossip, and rumors. The information presented in these letters is invaluable. Other than describing some of the major events of this period, the letters also offer details ranging from the weather and the types of diseases to prices of different goods and the daily meal. This wealth of news helps us to put things in context and provides us with a background that is often missing from sources, such as government documents or newspaper articles.[8]

In the following pages, we will discuss the main points contained in these letters, divided into different categories. This categorization is based on the content of the letters and also inspired by similar works in the past.[9] In addition, we will provide the historical context of the German occupation in Thessaloniki, so as to better frame this content. Last but not least, we will try to explain how these letters enrich our knowledge of that period and how they add to what we already know.

Nazi Measures against the Jews of Thessaloniki

In order to have the necessary context to place the letters from the three mothers, it is important to provide a brief historical overview of the

Nazi antisemitic measures against the Jews of Thessaloniki, which led to their deportation and extermination in Auschwitz. The Germans entered Thessaloniki in April 1941. At the beginning, there were no antisemitic actions that were systematic or exclusively touched the Jewish population. Surely, some Jewish leaders were imprisoned, the Jewish archives and libraries were confiscated, Jewish newspapers were shut down, and some Jewish merchants were forced to hand over the ownership of their companies. Yet, the majority of the Jews of Thessaloniki did not perceive them as an organized antisemitic campaign against them. These measures did not have a mass character, and most of the people went on with their lives, suffering as much as their Christian compatriots did.

The delay in the implementation of antisemitic policies in Thessaloniki could be explained by the German wish to apply uniformly the measures to all Jews in the country. That required the consent of the Italians, who were not willing to cooperate on that matter. The Jews were seen as agents of Italian culture, especially in the newly acquired territories for which they had preponderance. When the Germans realized that the Italians were not willing to collaborate, they decided to proceed unilaterally with the deportation of the Jews in the territories they controlled.[10]

The first mass measures against the Jews of Thessaloniki started to be implemented more than one year after the German invasion. On 11 July 1942, all male Jews aged between eighteen and forty-five were ordered to gather in the central Liberty Square to register for forced labor.[11] On that day, shocking scenes of public humiliation took place, with beatings and cries under a burning sun. It is pertinent to clarify that this measure was a local initiative rather than the result of an order that originated in Berlin.[12] During the weeks that followed, thousands of Jews were sent for hard construction works in different parts of Greece. Due to the heavy work, poor nutrition, and bad conditions, there was a high mortality rate, as these men were far from qualified.[13] In order to release the Jewish laborers, the Jewish Community had to agree to two painful demands: the collection of a ransom of two billion drachmas and, in addition, the destruction of the city's ancient Jewish cemetery, a process that started on 6 December 1942.

Two Jews, former members of the Greek Parliament, are among the victims of the German reprisals in Thessaloniki. Printer Michel Cazes, member of parliament of the United Front of 1932, was executed on 14 February 1942. David Soulam, MP of the same party in 1926, was executed on 30 December 1942.[14] They are the only members of the Greek Parliament who were targeted and killed by the foreign occupier. In the

Figure 0.2. Jewish men of Thessaloniki gathered in Liberty Square and forced to undergo humiliating gymnastics to register for forced labor. German soldiers stand in the back and watch. Source: Bundesarchiv.

middle of February 1943, the first phase of renaming the streets that bore Jewish names began. This was another measure aimed to remove signs of the city's Jewish character. This process was completed after several months.[15]

The arrival the same month of SS officers Dieter Wisliceny and Alois Brunner, sent by Adolf Eichmann, marked the beginning of the implementation of the "Final Solution" in Thessaloniki, which included harsh antisemitic measures. After 25 February 1943, Jews had to move to ghettos, which were set up for this reason.[16] All those who lived in other areas had to move to these designated areas, and several Jewish families often found themselves crammed together in one apartment. The Christian families who lived in the area could remain at their homes. In addition, the Jews were forced to wear a yellow star and declare all their possessions.

During the same period, the city's chamber of commerce and professional associations were ordered to remove all Jews from the membership, which meant that, from then on, Jews could not exercise any profession. Regrettably, most associations implemented this order immediately, without delaying the action or trying to stand by the persecuted Jews.[17]

Figure 0.3. A group of friends wearing the yellow star in the ghetto of Thessaloniki, March–April 1943. The second woman from the left is Alice Bivas, who perished at Auschwitz together with her parents. She sent this photograph to her family. Source: Archive of Liliane Arditti-Beizermann.

From the ghettos, the Jews would be transferred to the Baron Hirsch transit camp, a poor Jewish neighborhood in front of what was then the train station, which had been fenced and prepared for the occasion. After waiting there for two days, they were loaded in cattle cars under horrific conditions, eighty to one hundred people in each wagon, with little food and water and no sanitation, to be transported to the death camp of Auschwitz, in Nazi-occupied Poland, after a trip lasting several days. When the Hirsch camp was vacated, it would be filled by Jews from other districts.

The first transport of some twenty-five hundred Jews left Thessaloniki on 15 March 1943. In a telegram to Berlin, the German consul in Thessaloniki, Fritz Schönberg, reported:

> The evacuation of approximately 56,000 counted persons, local Jews with Greek citizenship, began today with the transportation of 2,600 persons from Salonika to the General Government [Occupied Poland]. The plan is to carry out four transports every week; thus, the entire operation will be completed in 6 weeks. The movable and immovable property of the evacuated Jews will

Figure 0.4. Transport of Jews from the ghetto in the eastern part of Thessaloniki to the Baron Hirsch transit camp, via Egnatia Street, 9 April 1943. The Jews can be seen in between two columns of onlookers who are watching the scene. The photo was taken from a balcony, where one can also see the father and sister of the photographer. Source: Archive of the Jewish Museum of Thessaloniki.

> be confiscated and transferred to a fund from which transport expenses and debts will be paid. The businesses of the evacuees will continue to be run by Greek trustees until further notice.[18]

After August 1943, virtually no Jew remained in the city, and after the end of the war, very few came back alive.

On 7 March 1943, the Agency for the Custody of Jewish Property (YDIP) was founded, with the goal to administer the vacated Jewish properties and thus offer a layer of legitimacy to their plunder, which was about to follow. The YDIP was in charge of registering Jewish properties (shops and apartments) and their contents and appointing Christian custodians. The Germans took for themselves a large part of the movable property, as did several of their local collaborators. A big part of the society, merchants, employers, refugees, state agencies, and associations, as well as German collaborators, took over the direction of the shops and businesses.[19]

The Use of Languages and Terms

All letters were written in cursive French. Most letters are two pages long (one double-paged sheet), and more rarely three or four pages (two sheets). Sometimes, other people—brother, aunt—added some words at the end of the letters. The level of their French was high, with a few grammatical typos or spelling errors, although they may not have reread and corrected the text due to stress or shortage of time. The women's knowledge of French indicates that they came from middle-class families who were able to afford high school education for their daughters.

To understand the significance of the French language to the Jewish community of Thessaloniki at the time, it is important to recall the network of Alliance Israélite Universelle schools, which tried to introduce Western educational norms among the Jews in Southeast Europe and the wider region.[20] The first girls' school in Thessaloniki was founded in September 1874.[21] French was the main language of instruction in the schools, both for boys and also for girls.[22] According to Eyal Ginio, French "represented . . . the enlightened and redeeming culture of the West." It was therefore the language of choice for all correspondence, be it business or personal.[23]

Another aspect with regard to the language of the correspondence is the use of Judeo-Spanish, transcribed in Latin letters. Ginio explained that Judeo-Spanish was used for more familiar or informal discussion, and while "no longer regarded as a respectful and modern means of communication, it continued, nevertheless, to serve as a language of intimate conversation."[24] The role of Judeo-Spanish as a mother tongue among the Jewish families of Thessaloniki had changed over time.[25] After the integration of Thessaloniki into the Greek state in 1912, a young generation of Thessaloniki Jews was taught Greek as their first language in both the community and the state-run schools. This new reality made the use of Judeo-Spanish gradually more infrequent.[26] The mothers used the Spanish Jewish idiom to varying degrees. For example, Mathilde Barouh, when describing the harsh realities in the ghetto and her personal suffering, often reverted to Judeo-Spanish—her mother tongue—not formal French.

In addition, all three mothers used few Greek words, mostly in Latin script and rarely in Greek alphabet, for terms that related to the special vocabulary of the period, such as *politofilakas* (Jewish civilian guard at the ghetto), *sissition* (daily food allowance), etc. Although they had not gone to Greek schools, they sometimes utilized in their letters Greek expressions translated into French. This shows an increased exposure to Greek culture and language, despite the fact that they wrote in French or may not have used the Greek alphabet regularly.

In general, the three mothers wrote to their sons openly, without an apparent use of code words to refer to certain people. As the situation deteriorated, however, they sometimes used initials or indirect ways to refer to people, probably in an effort to protect their identities in case the letters were intercepted. Such are mentions like "your friend," "your two acquaintances," or "the gentleman you wrote to me about." Some of these cryptic references to people may also be due to the familiarity they had with them. Interestingly, Neama Cazes stopped writing the names of her children as the antisemitic measures were intensifying. On 19 March 1943, four days after the first train had left Thessaloniki, Ms. Cazes began her letter with "My dear Maurice" for the last time. From 24 March, they started with "My dear children." She also used the Greek name "Aleco" when referring to her son "Alberto." Similarly, in her last letters, Sara Saltiel did not mention by name her son's two Christian schoolmates and close friends.

The language used in the letters gives us a great insight into the linguistic reality of that period for Thessaloniki's Jews. French remained the language of formal correspondence. It was infused with Judeo-Spanish and Greek, when the former gradually ceded its place to the latter as the main spoken language of the Jewish community. The choice of words, and whether to mention specific names or not, demonstrates the awareness of the three mothers to the rapidly deteriorating situation, which required careful attention and more secrecy.

Narration of Everyday Life

The rising prices and the constant depreciation of the drachma made the life of the people of Thessaloniki very difficult, and it affected their daily nutrition. The three mothers, like the rest of the residents, had to face the many difficulties of this period, including limited food supplies, lack of heating, and great uncertainty. In the letters, we find information on the daily meals, the availability of foodstuffs, and the different recipes. They also referred to the different goods in the market and their prices. In these conditions, it is only natural that local transportation was also affected, with the price of a tram ticket on the rise. Many then opted to go to their jobs on foot, or to not go to the city center at all, although the trams appeared full, maybe because they had reduced circulation.

The hunger affected a large percentage of the population and caused a lot of deaths. In Thessaloniki, the famine is estimated to have lasted from December 1941 to March 1943, and an outbreak of malaria exacerbated it.[27] According to Maria Kavala, the deaths in Thessaloniki due to famine were about 1 percent of the total population, i.e. 1,785 people, of whom 773 (43.3 percent) were Jews, two times higher in relation to the Christian population.[28] Using different sources, the Jewish Museum of Thessaloniki speaks of Jewish deaths three times higher than those of Greek Christians in 1942.[29] The International Red Cross estimated that between 1943 and 1944, 98 percent of the population of Thessaloniki and its outskirts, some 285,000 people on average, were in need of food aid.[30]

In the letters, we read about a poor domestic aid and an older lady, both of them described as "skeletons." This also matches the description that most of the victims of famine were from the lower classes or elderly.[31] Under these circumstances, the Jewish Community took on even more responsibilities, realizing the vulnerability of its constituency. A coordinating committee for social welfare, composed of prominent members of the community, had been created in April 1942, and the challenges they had to tackle were constantly increasing.[32] Soup kitchens for children were also in operation, which grew from two thousand recipients in April 1942 to fifty-five hundred in the middle of October, a number that swelled even more rapidly during the first months of 1943.[33]

During the same period, robberies increased significantly, and the mothers describe such events. This phenomenon must be linked to the difficult economic situation, which drove many to these illegal acts. Such descriptions remind us of the widespread poverty during this period and the value of items, such as a blanket or a woolen shirt.

From the letters, mainly of Sara Saltiel, the reader can glean information regarding the cultural life of the city and how the citizens spent their leisure time prior to the ghettoization. Due to the cold and the increased food prices during the winter of 1942–43, it was often the case that people visited each other's homes, mostly the warmest among family members and friends. There, they chatted, played cards, or even sang and danced. Ms. Saltiel went regularly to concerts and to the cinema. In the letters, she described many of these events and her impressions. In the summer of 1942, they swam in the sea or took an occasional boat ride. In the winter, when the weather was good, they preferred walks by the seafront or parks with friends, as well as small excursions.

The war situation did limit social events, such as weddings or bar mitzvah ceremonies. As the food was scarce and expensive, invitations and big spending were avoided. Most people preferred to postpone the celebrations until after the war and to accept invitations at home or do absolutely nothing. Nevertheless, some festive events did take place, especially among the more affluent members, such as the marriage of Leon J. Cohen to Germaine Perahia, daughter of banker Jessua Perahia, in January 1943, which is described in the letters.

Formal and Informal Relations between Jews and Non-Jews: Family Members, Friends, and Neighbors

The letters from the three mothers offer a glimpse of their daily interactions with family, friends, and neighbors, both Jewish and Christian. Interpersonal relations are a very important element, especially in times of crisis, like during World War II, when support networks were crucial. These relationships between Jews and Christians, although challenged due to the circumstances, were not contained strictly along religious lines but had a lot of cordial elements, at least in the central areas where the three mothers resided.

Family members were very close in order to deal with the hardships of the period and to provide support, but they also kept each other company. Ms. Saltiel did her best to keep her family well during these difficult times. Her in-laws sometimes stayed with her and her husband in the apartment. She often invited relatives for dinner. She tried to cheer people up, even though she sometimes felt the urge to cry. The difficulties of the period put strains on her relationship her husband. Ms. Saltiel complained that he would return home from work troubled and not in the mood for any conversation. She spoke of her "solitude" and wrote to her son that his letters were the one thing that would console her. The other two mothers, Mathilde Barouh and Neama Cazes, were widows whose children lived in Athens. As a result, they had to rely on extended families or acquaintances. Ms. Barouh stayed with her sister, while Ms. Cazes did not have any close family members in her home.

Another important element is the interaction with their non-Jewish friends and neighbors. In the letters, we see a quite close relation between Jews and non-Jews, which went beyond the traditional dividing lines. Sara Saltiel was very close to her son's Christian friends, some of whom were studying with him in Athens. In fact, her son Maurice moved into the house of the grandmother of Sotiris Faltsis, one of his best friends. Ms. Saltiel saw her son's friends regularly, and through them she and her son sent clothes, food, and other supplies back and forth to Athens. She also gave them gifts, visited them when they were sick, invited them for dinner, went to the cinema with them, and met up socially with their parents.

The Saltiel family had a wide circle of business partners and acquaintances who were Christians. Mr. Saltiel's Christian business partners would sometimes spend the night at their home. There were also several people, such as acquaintances and friends of friends, through which Sara Saltiel used to send things to her son. At the time, their relations appeared to be cordial and sincere, seemingly unaffected by the antisemitic propaganda, German measures, and anti-Jewish restrictions of the period. Ms. Barouh also mentioned names of Greek Christians, but she did not indicate that they had a very close relationship. Two Christian acquaintances visited her in the ghetto during the time of the deportations in order to pass on information to her from her family in Athens. Ms. Cazes, too, described her relations with Christians, commercial contacts, or acquaintances, of whom some appeared somewhat cautious, however.

These cordial relations between Jews and non-Jews reveal an unknown aspect of the everyday life in Thessaloniki during the period of the German occupation. Due to the general lack of other contemporary sources, the letters shed a light into the state of intercommunal relations and open the way for more research on the issue.

Narration of Anti-Jewish Measures

The mothers offer a unique eyewitness insight into the anti-Jewish measures that took place in Thessaloniki during the German occupation. In the beginning, the three women were careful not to paint a dark picture to their children. This could be due to the fact that they did not want their sons to worry too much, but it could also be because they hoped the situation would remain stable—or even improve—and that these were isolated incidents. Nevertheless, as they witnessed the antisemitic measures gradually intensifying and the situation deteriorating at an increasing pace, their accounts became more emotional and blunt, with little hope or optimism.

Sara Saltiel's flat was requisitioned by the Germans, and subsequently in 1942 she had to change apartments several times while looking for more permanent housing. The furniture, after being confiscated, was returned to the family in a very bad condition. She became worried as the winter months approached that she would not be able to find a new place to live. Her troubles with housing seemed endless, and she was actively searching for a new home for some time. She was so desperate that she went to a medium to seek some clarity. In October 1942, she moved to a flat that was far from desirable and with very bad sanitary conditions, having been left with no choice.

The gathering in Liberty Square on 11 July 1942—in order to register Jewish males for forced labor—was not mentioned in the letters, but its repercussions were. Ms. Saltiel described these developments to her son, specifying family friends or relatives who were drafted for these works. In some households no man was left behind, while in others, those who were sick would be sent to the works once their situation improved. When some of the workers returned from the forced labor camps in mid-October 1942, Sara Saltiel described their poor condition and the diseases many of them carried. At this point, only the sick were allowed to return to Thessaloniki, and the Community began to collect the ransom of two billion drachmas in order to release the rest of the workers. A committee of the Jewish Community came up with lists of how much each member should contribute based on their financial background.[34] There is no mention in the letters of the destruction of the old Jewish cemetery of the city, which commenced on 6 December 1942 and was part of the deal.

In February 1943, the Saltiels were forced to undergo the German restrictions. They had to reside in particular areas, with many families in one apartment. From this point on, Ms. Saltiel broke down emotionally and could not restrain her tears and agony due to the great adversities and uncertainty they were experiencing. The other two mothers wrote the letters to their sons with crying eyes and trembling hand. All three described the life in the ghetto with the darkest of colors. Even though they do not mention the obligation to wear the yellow star, they do refer to personal experiences and incidents.

Life in the Ghetto and Personal Emotional State

The letters from the three mothers are the only primary contemporary source that offers a perspective into the life in the ghettos of Thessaloniki. Through them, one can learn the severe impact of these anti-Jewish measures on the Jewish population of Thessaloniki, such as the restrictions in circulation,[35] the closure of businesses, and the registration of properties. The ghettos had been closed, and exit was allowed only with a special permit. They were guarded by the Greek police and a special Jewish unit that was formed for that purpose.[36] At the same time, the Greek Christian families who resided in the area remained in their homes, living side-by-side with the Jewish families without having to undergo the same restrictions.

The three mothers were located in different parts of Thessaloniki. The Saltiel family was residing in the ghetto of the city center, over Egnatias Avenue, on Ptolemeon 43. Ms. Barouh and Ms. Cazes lived in the big ghetto in the eastern part of the city, and their homes where they wrote their last letters before their deportation were Amalias 30 and Deligiorgi 33 respectively.

The situation took a very heavy toll on the Jewish population. The people inside the ghetto had to live with the daily fear of deportation. They struggled with adapting to the new reality, accepting it as the new standard, while preparing for the trip to an unknown future. They did not know when they would depart and lived a constant torment of uncertainty and anxiety. These circumstances caused grave emotional consequences, and many endured extreme psychological pressure without an end in sight. The fact that they had no jobs, income, or any other occupation exacerbated their already critical living situation. Hunger, poverty, anxiety, and uncertainty crushed them. In the letters, we see the three mothers in a very poor emotional and psychological state. They had feelings of hopelessness and self-pity, they were demoralized, and they spoke of a state of panic and agony. There was also a sense of acceptance, of leaving things to destiny, that things simply "were written" this way.

With the deportations on the horizon, the letters describe the efforts of the people to sell their personal belongings, with ruthless merchants walking the streets of the ghetto waiting to buy everything for a small fee or a little food. The mothers seem to despair, as nothing belonged to them anymore, and their household that they had built for so long had no value.

In the ghetto, there was a surge in marriage rates, reinforced by rumors that married couples would get their own house at the new destination.[37] Wedding ceremonies increased exponentially with couples getting married in large groups, with some of the partners only getting to know each other a few hours before the nuptials. Dowry and a big ceremony were the least of their worries. Some unfortunate ones could not get married in the wake of their partner being deported before the wedding could take place. Others could not because their future partner had a foreign passport, and marriages with people of other nationalities were forbidden.[38] Interestingly, there was a rise of divorces in the ghettos, possibly due to couples not wishing to remain together during the difficult times.[39]

The letters describe the preparations for the long journey to Poland. To be able to carry their personal effects, along with babies, the elderly, and the sick, several people would buy small carts that they loaded and parked in front of their door. Concerning luggage, they could only take with them a small bag of twenty kilos per person, with the most basic belongings. No suitcases were allowed.[40] For this reason they would prepare a backpack, which they would have ready by their bed.

In the letters there is a clear sense of doom, that their final days were approaching. The mothers felt deep emotions of hopelessness, although some rays of hope occasionally crept in, when they prayed for a miracle or the chance to reunite with their children. Their profound love for and affection toward their children is omnipresent in the writings of all three. Their sons tried to help their mothers as much as they could. They asked Christian friends or acquaintances to visit their mothers in their homes. This was often the only contact they had with the outside world, and through the visitors they sent messages to their children. Their sons, living in relative freedom and safety in Athens, were possibly the only positive thought they had left to cling to. Their sons were always on their minds, offering them emotional and mental support and giving them courage to endure the challenges they faced.

Finally, it is important to add that in the letters from the three women there were no emotions of hate or revenge against the Germans, not even a reference to them.[41] Similarly, references to any responsibilities of the community leadership or the Greek authorities are also absent.

Deportation and Options for Escape

The three mothers, with their families and friends, were deported and murdered in Auschwitz. They remained in the ghetto while the first trains started leaving Thessaloniki to German-occupied Poland, transporting the Jews from the poorer neighborhoods close to the train station. They must have been deported to the unknown destination shortly after they sent their last letters to their sons.

The three authors described the procedure of the deportations in heartbreaking detail. The reactions of the people the day of the departure are shocking. The inhuman conditions on the deportation trains were known to them, and the mere thought of the journey would freeze their blood. They worried about the elderly and sick, but also about themselves, that they would not come out of the journey alive. The wait inside the ghetto until the date of the departure was nerve-racking. People could not sleep at night and laid in bed with their clothes on to be ready. For some of them, the departure would signal the end of their suffering in the ghetto, since the transfer to Poland was unavoidable.

While the nature of the final destination—a factory of death set up to exterminate them—was unknown to them, the three mothers had a sense of the very precarious situation they were in. The context of the war, the daily life in the ghetto with all its hardships, and in particular the way the deportations were being carried out all signaled the gravity and seriousness of their condition. The severe parameters of their displacement were becoming apparent to them, not by concrete words or exact information but by actions, observation, and emotions. Facing these adversities—and possibly foreseeing their immediate future—they had few doubts about what would happen to them. They used expressions such as "death," "extermination," "last hour," "fatal moment," and "condemned to death sentence." The situation around them did not give them any hope for encouragement or optimism.

Before this escalation of the situation—and possibly predicting their immediate future—the three mothers each tried to find a way to escape. Leaving Thessaloniki and joining their children in Athens would be a logical decision. One of their sons tried to issue a permit so that his mother could travel to Athens. They were not successful, and the German authorities would not accept such documents. Some appealed to the Italian consulate, which had a positive attitude toward the persecuted Jews,[42] but were not successful there either. The option of a wedding with a foreign citizen could also have been a solution. Unfortunately for them, their efforts were fruitless, and they could not escape the deportation and murder in Auschwitz.

The descriptions the three mothers gave of the situation in the ghetto, the options of escape, and the stance of the Jewish population touch the broader debate related to the presumed passivity of the victims. Could more Jews of Thessaloniki have been saved during this period of persecution? The letters offer us some important elements, which could serve as an impetus for more comprehensive research. At the same time, detailed sources on the thinking of the Jewish leadership are lacking,[43] or even on the stance of the youth, who could have escaped easier or organized some resistance.

The situation deteriorated at a rapid pace, a fact that did not help the reflexes of the persecuted Jews. The three mothers were not young, and it was not easy for them to escape. Their age, language, accent, and the lack of connections with the resistance or people in the countryside were factors that worked against them. They had large families in a traditional society, where reckless attempts or taking risks were not generally accepted. Their circle of loved ones included sick individuals, the elderly, pregnant women, and small children. To escape and leave them behind without support was not an easy thing.

Most of the Jews of Thessaloniki belonged to an urban population, with limited networks outside the city. Many were active in trade, managing businesses or shops with a lot of merchandise and capital invested in them. In the letters, there are many references to interpersonal relations with Christians, but nothing on escape networks or offers to hide in Christian homes. It is possible that these existed but were not recorded.

When the three mothers finally realized the true nature of the persecution, it was already too late—they were imprisoned in the ghetto. Their only chances of escape were via peaceful, legal means, such as moving to Athens or marrying a foreign subject. In general, there are almost no references to organized mass reactions of the authorities of Thessaloniki or the ordinary people, no protests, complaints, or acts of solidarity. Only three cases are known of Jewish families who hid in Christian homes in the city of Thessaloniki during the whole period of the German occupation.[44]

Approaches to Faith, Relation with God

Thessaloniki was traditionally a very important Jewish religious center. However, at the beginning of the twentieth century, religious observance was decreasing. Thessaloniki scholar Joseph Nehama described a society that was more secular and tolerant, attributing it to reasons such as education and analytical thinking, the big fire of 1917 that destroyed much of the religious infrastructure, the decline of the religious authorities, and the participation in the social life of the lower classes.[45] Following this general pattern, the three mothers do not seem to be very religious. They were probably traditional, observing the different religious customs and the Jewish High Holidays.

Despite their lack of observance of official religious practice, the three mothers displayed a spiritual faith in God. In the difficult circumstances in which they found themselves, God became a way out for them, and they prayed and hoped for a better future. God was the only support that they had left, that gave them hope and strength to continue. They asked God for a miracle that would bring them back to the prior calm and peaceful situation and allow them to see their children again. Prayer and faith in God became their only consolation in the face of the difficult voyage toward the unknown that awaited them. This also showed the irreversible situation they were in, as they could not find help or assistance from anywhere else. In addition, the three mothers opened themselves to their sons. They spoke about their lives, recording in their letters a kind of reckoning of their actions until then. They tried to be kind and helpful to others and hoped that God would reward them for that.

Final Words to Their Children

As the time of the deportation approached for the three mothers, the tone of their letters increased in emotion. Their writings were a means to communicate their last words to their children, to offer advice, and to share their last requests. They tried to pass on to their sons their wisdom and blessings, words that they would usually save for important life events, such as their wedding day.

Some of the mothers mentioned the people who stood by their side during these difficult hours, so that their sons knew and could repay them one day. They advised them which people to trust and who they should keep by their side for the rest of their lives. They reassured them that they would also be loved and welcomed by their adopted families. They indicated where they had left some things for them and where they would meet after the war was over.

Starting in the beginning of March 1943, the mothers began offering prayers and blessings for their sons. They wished them health and a bright future and prayed to God to protect them. They asked them to be kind and generous with everyone and to be careful of the ones that tried to take advantage of them. The mothers worried about what would happen to their sons if the anti-Jewish measures would expand also in Athens, which would put their children in danger. In that case, they advised them to get rid of their possessions and acquire cash so that they could deal with the difficult circumstances.

The letters from the three mothers contain a unique characteristic, expressing a universal message of love, hope, and peace. The very loaded phrases contained in the final letters served as their final testament to the sons, as the three mothers realized their end was approaching. They offered their blessings, pieces of advice, as well as their last kiss and goodbye. They reiterated their love to their children and their hope of seeing them again. Finally, they expressed their wish that their children would not forget them.

Notes

1. Molho and Nehama, *In Memoriam*. The book was first published in French.
2. For an overview of the historiography of the Holocaust in Greece, see, for example, Avloniti, "Holocaust"; Benveniste, "Istoriografia"; Benveniste, "Coming Out"; A. Molho, "Introduction"; R. Molho, *Olokautoma*, 25–48; and Varon-Vassard, "Genoktonia."
3. Yacoel, *Apomnimoneumata*. Yacoel's diary is also available in English in Bowman, *Holocaust in Salonika*, 25–122. Yacoel was writing his diary while hidden in Athens between 1943 and 1944, before he was arrested and deported.
4. See for example Apostolou, "Exception"; Fleischer, *Stemma kai Svastiga*, 296–348; Margaritis, *Anepithimitoi Sympatriotes*; Mazower, *Salonica*, 392–411; Ritzaleos, "Elliniki Orthodoxi Ekklisia."
5. Molho and Nehama, *In Memoriam*, 116.
6. The stamp reads "Ufficio Censura Postale Atene" and the banner "Verificato Per Censura." Envelopes from January and February 1943 do not bear any marks. No other envelopes have been found.
7. On 10 January 1943, an announcement of the German commander of Thessaloniki published in the local press called for people to use the phone only in urgent cases and to avoid any unnecessary conversations. In case the monthly quota was exceeded, the owner was threatened with losing the telephone connection and further punishment. *Nea Evropi* [New Europe], 10 January 1943. This order may have discouraged many people from using the telephone.
8. There were two newspapers in circulation in Thessaloniki during this period, *Nea Evropi* [New Europe] and *Apogevmatini* [Evening], both run by Greek collaborators of the Nazis. For more background on the collaboration press of Thessaloniki, see Patrikiou, "Mia 'Nea' Istoriki Periodos" and Dordanas "Ehthros me tin Pena."
9. See for example Bacharach, *Last Letters*.
10. Dublon-Knebel, *German Foreign Office*, 24. See also other relevant documents in the volume.
11. These measures did not apply to Jews of Italian citizenship or those of neutral states.
12. For more on these events, see Saltiel, *Holocaust*, 47–56.
13. For the mortality rate, Yacoel gives a figure of 3 percent in two and a half months. This would be approximately 100 people. Yacoel, *Apomnimoneumata*, 71. Molho misquotes Yacoel and gives a rate of 12 percent. Molho and Nehama, *In Memoriam*, 69. In fact, Molho must have confused it with a 12 that appeared close by in Yacoel's text but was unrelated. In his 1961 deposition to the Eichmann trial, German officer Max Merten said that there "was a high mortality rate, and I consider that the figure of twelve percent in two and a half months, given by Michael Molho in his book *In Memoriam*, is still too low" ("Testimony"). Merten may have claimed that the rate was

even higher than 12 percent to bolster his humanitarian actions for his defense. We believe Yacoel's is a more plausible figure.

14. Dodos, *Ebraioi tis Thessalonikis*, 264.
15. Tsironis, "Onomatothesies kai Metonomasies," 190–93 and Saltiel, *Holocaust*, 107–10.
16. For more on the ghettos established in Thessaloniki see Hadar, "Space and Time"; Hekimoglou, "Exact Location"; R. Molho, *Olokautoma* 69–71, United States Holocaust Memorial Museum, *Encyclopedia*, 1941–48.
17. Saltiel, *Holocaust*, 151–64.
18. Dublon-Knebel, *German Foreign Office*, telegram T50, Schönberg to Berlin, 15 March 1943, 120.
19. See for example Dordanas, "Exontosi kai Leilasia."
20. R. Molho, *Ebraioi tis Thessalonikis*, 142–46.
21. R. Molho, "Education," 262.
22. R. Molho, *Ebraioi tis Thessalonikis*, 175–79.
23. Ginio, "Learning," 236.
24. Ibid.
25. Bunis, "Salonika."
26. Molho and Nehama, *In Memoriam*, 20–21, and Naar, *Jewish Salonica*, 156–88.
27. For more on the hunger see Hionidou, *Famine and Death*; Clogg, *Bearing Gifts*; and Kavala, "Epiviosi."
28. Kavala, "Thessaloniki," 182–91.
29. "Divided Memories 1940–1950: Between History and Experience," exhibition, Macedonian Museum of Contemporary Art, Thessaloniki, December 2016–February 2017, quoting a study of "medical doctor Athanasios Mantekos (1903–2006) an international personality in the field of public health."
30. Helger, *Ravitaillement*, 323.
31. Kavala, "Epiviosi," 17.
32. Yacoel was the de facto leader of this group. On its creation, see Yacoel, *Apomnimoneumata*, 51–52.
33. Archive of the Jewish Museum of Thessaloniki, Box 9, Subseries 2: Correspondence of Matanoth Laevionim, File 165: Correspondence regarding Mess Halls of Thessaloniki and related items, 1940–1943.
34. See Yacoel, *Apomnimoneumata*, 78–83.
35. Prohibition of circulation after sunset. This measure was announced to Chief Rabbi Koretz by the SS on 8 February 1943, with the date of implementation of 25 February. See Yacoel, *Apomnimoneumata*, 101.
36. The Germans ordered the Community to prepare a corps of 250 Jews, preferably young, who would be auxiliaries to the Community, under orders by the SS. See Yacoel, *Apomnimoneumata*, 116, and Molho and Nehama, *In Memoriam*, 92.
37. For more on the marriages in the ghetto, see Hadar, "Marriage," and Molho and Nehama, *In Memoriam,* 115–16.
38. This was due to the fact that Jews of certain foreign citizenships were exempt from the measures. See order 1237 of 6 February 1943, provided in Molho and Nehama, *In Memoriam*, 84–85, with the German original on page 163.
39. Historical Archive of the Jewish Community of Thessaloniki, Letter of Sarina Sides, 31 March 1943.
40. Molho and Nehama, *In Memoriam*, 108.
41. For a discussion on the absence of reference to the German perpetrators in Holocaust victims' diaries, see Tahvonen, "Perpetrators and Possibilities," 110–19.
42. For a review of the role of the Italian consulate in Thessaloniki in helping the Jews, see Carpi, *Italian Diplomatic Documents*.

43. Such references are lacking, and the narration in Yacoel's diary ends before the beginning of the deportations.
44. These families were Algava, Assael, and Pardo. The son of the first family published his memoirs: Algava, *600 Days in Hiding*. A daughter of the second family published her memoirs after the war: Ingram, *Unaccounted For*. Finally, a daughter of the third family published the diary she was keeping as a young teenager: Asser Pardo, *548 Days*.
45. Nehama, *Istoria*, 1592. Molho made similar observations as to the small number of religious leaders and the decreasing quality of religious education. Molho and Nehama, *In Memoriam*, 23–24.

INSTRUCTIONES

A LOS DJIDIOS EMIGRANDO DE THESSALONIKI

Los coreligionnarios preparandossen para la partencia deven tomar con si las cosas las mas indispensavles por el viaje, como tambien por el segiorno en el nuevo lugar de residencia sea:

1) Covierturas, moudadonras limpias, resias condourias y vestimientas solidas. Cosas de lusso son superfluas.

2) Comanias ke non se bosean son a preferar. Se deve tomar tambien con si una gourde o una redoma para la agua.

3) La [illegible] y la [illegible] deven ser bien empaquetadas en una valija o tchanta y las comanias en otra tchanta.

4) Las paras en drachmes non pouеden ser tomadas con si. Deven ser remettidas al Baron Hirsch, a la Commission communala y convertidas en zlotys. Akel ke, malgrade esto, toma con si drachmes por el viaje, se exposa a una severa punition.

5) Todo el oro, djoyas y qualunke otro objeto de valor topandosse en possession del partiente, deven ser remettidos a la Commission Communala, la quala enregistrara estos objetos por ser remettidos a la Communita.

6) Antes de la partencia, se deve remetter las yaves de la grouta, en el cavso ande non se topan en poder del messengiouhos, a la Communita.

7) Mientres el segiorno al Baron Hirsch como mientres el embarcamiento por la partencia, se deve guadrar el orden y suivir las recommandaciones de la Politofilaki y de los miembros de la Commission preposados a este effeto.

8) Se recommenda de ayoudar y de [illegible] mientres el embarcamiento como tambien mientres el viaje, a los hazinos, aviadados, mujeres y criaturas.

9) Por el approvisiounamiento en comanias mientres el viaje, [illegible] la Communita Djudia de Thessaloniki. [illegible] se topar las comanias [illegible] bastantes para todo el viaje.

10) Se recommenda de respectar, [illegible] el viaje, los ordenes del sur-[illegible], cargado de assegurar el orden y [illegible] justa esparticion de las comanias.

Thessaloniki, el 6 Avril 1943

El Presidente de la Communita Djudia y Gran-Rabbino de Thessaloniki

Dr. Savy Koretz

Prologue

Instructions to Jews Migrating from Thessaloniki

The coreligionists who are preparing for the departure must take with them the most indispensable items for the trip, as well as for the stay in the new place of residency, such as:

1. Blankets, clean underwear, strong shoes, and solid clothes. Luxury items are superfluous.
2. Foods that do not perish are preferable. You should also take a flask or a bottle for water.
3. The clothes and underwear have to be packed well in a suitcase or bag and the foodstuffs in another bag.
4. The money in drachmas cannot be taken with you. They have to be deposited at Baron Hirsch, at the Communal Commission and be converted to zlotys. Despite this, whoever takes drachmas for this trip will face a severe punishment.
5. All the gold, jewelry, and any other object of value in the possession of the departing has to be deposited at the Communal Commission, who will register these objects to be given to the Community.
6. Before the departure, the keys of the store have to be given to the Community, in case they are not in the possession of the custodian.
7. During the stay at the Baron Hirsch as well as during the boarding for the departure, you have to keep the order and follow the recom-

mendations of the Civilian Guards and the members of the Commission designated to that effect.

8. It is recommended that you help and console the sick, the elderly, the women, and children during the boarding and also during the trip.
9. For the provisioning of food during the journey, the Jewish Community of Thessaloniki has made arrangements so that the food can last for the whole tip.
10. It is recommended to respect, during the trip, the orders of the supervisor of each wagon, who is in charge of ensuring the order and the fair division of the food.

Thessaloniki, 6 April 1943
The President of the Jewish Community and
Chief Rabbi of Thessaloniki
Dr. Sevy Koretz

Archive of the Jewish Museum of Thessaloniki

List of Letters

Sara Saltiel Letters

Date	Number of pages	Author
4 January 1942	2	Irene Marcos
17 May 1942	2	Sara Saltiel
26 May 1942	2	Sara Saltiel
17 August 1942	2	Sara Saltiel
[25 August 1942]	2	Sara Saltiel
[beginning September 1942]	1	Sara Saltiel
10 September 1942	2	Sara Saltiel
14 [September] 1942	2	Sara Saltiel
20 September 1942	2	Irene Marcos
21 September 1942	2	Sara Saltiel
[1 October 1942]	2	Sara Saltiel
8 October 1942	2	Sara Saltiel
18 October 1942	2	Sara Saltiel
27 October 1942	2	Sara Saltiel
1 November 1942	2	Sara Saltiel
26 November 1942	2	Sara Saltiel
2 December 1942	2	Sara Saltiel
11 December 1942	2	Sara Saltiel

Date	Number of pages	Author
17 December 1942	2	Sara Saltiel
27 December 1942	2	Sara Saltiel
3 January 1943	2	Sara Saltiel
18 January 1943	2	Sara Saltiel
26 January 1943	2	Sara Saltiel
1 February 1943	2	Sara Saltiel
8 February 1943	2	Sara Saltiel
9 February 1943	1	Sara Saltiel
23 February 1943	2	Sara Saltiel
[beginning March] 1943	2	Sara Saltiel
17 March 1943	4	Sara Saltiel
21 March 1943	4	Sara Saltiel
[beginning April 1943]	2	Zak Serrero

Mathilde Barouh Letters

Date	Number of pages	Author
4 January 1943	1	Mathilde Barouh*
28 February 1943	2+1	Mathilde Barouh*
15 March 1943	3	Mathilde Barouh
18 March 1943	2	Mathilde Barouh
23 March 1943	2	Mathilde Barouh
1 April 1943	3	Mathilde Barouh
4 April 1943	2	Mathilde Barouh
7 April 1943	2	Mathilde Barouh
10 April 1943	4	Mathilde Barouh
13 April 1943	4	Mathilde Barouh and aunt
mid-April 1943	1	Mathilde Barouh
17 April 1943	1	Mathilde Barouh
25 May/7 June 1943	1	Fredy Barouh and Albertos*

Neama Cazes Letters

Date	Number of Pages	Author
29 January 1943	2	Neama Cazes*
30 January 1943	2	Berto Cazes
3 February 1943	2	Neama Cazes
4 February 1943	2	Berto Cazes
7 February 1943	2	Neama Cazes*
9 February 1943	1	Berto Cazes*
11 February 1943	2	Neama Cazes
13 February 1943	1	Berto Cazes
20 February 1943	4	Neama Cazes
21 February 1943	1	Neama Cazes
18 March 1943	2	Neama Cazes
19 March 1943	2	Neama Cazes
24 March 1943	1	Neama Cazes
27 March 1943	2	Neama Cazes
1 April 1943	2	Neama Cazes
4 [April] 1943	2	Neama Cazes
8 [April] 1943	2	Neama Cazes
9 April 1943	1	Maurice Cazes*
10 April 1943	2	Neama Cazes
13 April 1943	4	Maurice-Berto Cazes*

*These letters were found after the Greek edition was published.

Part I

Saltiel Letters

INTRODUCTION

Eleni Saltiel

Seventy-seven years have passed since March 1943, when the trip and final end of the family of Maurice Saltiel started. His mother, father, grandfather, grandmother, uncles, and cousins with their babies were exterminated in Auschwitz. The letters from Sarina to her son were left behind, which Maurice saved as a treasure in an old folder with the title "The Letters of My Mother."

Many years ago, Maurice gave them to me to read, and I was shaken. Since then, I have read and reread them, without any thoughts for publication. I consider them as a valuable family heirloom, exclusively ours. One of these letters was published in 2008 in *Maurice of Techni and of Art*, the book commemorating the ten-year anniversary of Maurice's death, which was read by Leon Saltiel. He was the one who thought to publish this book, and he encouraged me with enthusiasm, because the testimonies from the ghetto are scarce. We discussed it with Simos, my son, and decided that we had the duty to make this story known. I undertook the translation of the letters from French into Greek for the Greek edition, keeping the style and emotional load of the communication between the mother and her beloved son.

Sara (diminutive Sarina) Serrero, the mother of Maurice, was born in Thessaloniki in 1902. Her parents were David and Gracia. She studied at the French school of Alliance Française and became a teacher; she was also a pretty lady and talented, and she played the piano, often accompanying Maurice, who played the violin, in family concerts.

Figure 1.1. Sarina Serrero Saltiel. Archive of Eleni Saltiel.

Figure 1.2. Isaak, Sarina, and Maurice Saltiel, at a young age, in the spa town of Karlsbad. Archive of Eleni Saltiel.

She sewed her own clothes on a mannequin that she had in her own size; she was very elegant and liked to be photographed. Some photographs have survived with Maurice from family holidays and trips.

She sang very beautifully, and that was one of the reasons that Isaak (her husband) initially fell in love with her, when he heard her sing during a holiday.

Maurice adored her. He remembered from one of their trips to Karlsbad that in the synagogue they commemorated the memory of the great Jewish poet Haim Bialik, and his mother sang a song with lyrics written by the poet. Everybody was touched.

Isaak, Maurice's father, was a smart, energetic, and active man, a commercial genius. Together with his two brothers, they opened a shop of imported textiles on Vilara Street along with two additional branches, one on Venizelos Street and one in Vardaris. Isaak's parents were Mois Saltiel and Rahil Alvo.

Isaak and Sara got married in March 1921. They lived on Ionos Dragoumi Street (then Megalou Alexandrou). Later, they moved to Palaion Patron Germanou 31. During the German occupation, they changed residency often, every time that the Germans would requisition the apartment.

At home, they would speak French and Judeo-Spanish (Ladino). The traveled in the summers to spa towns in Europe, where Sarina took lessons in phonetics.

Maurice, an only child, was born in Thessaloniki in 1922 and studied first at De La Salle and the Valagianni schools and later at the Second Boys High School. From a young age, he took violin lessons, played the piano, and improvised. There are many cassette tapes with his improvisations. He studied economics at the University of Athens.

In February 1943, the Germans forced all the Jews of Thessaloniki to wear the yellow star with a number. Sarina and Isaak had numbers 7116 and 7117.

That same year, Maurice, who was located in Thessaloniki, returned to Athens, and with the advice of his father, rented in the name of Sotiris Faltsis, his classmate and family friend, a warehouse in the Matala arcade, where they transferred merchandise to avoid confiscation by the German authorities. In September 1943, following a denunciation, the Germans broke into the warehouse, took all the merchandise, and transported it in eight big trucks to an unknown address (a police statement exists dated 21 November 1944).

Maurice had initially hidden in Neochori of Halkidiki, in the home of the family of his classmate Vassilis Papamoschou (1920–2006). At one point, his presence became an issue in the village, and he had to leave.

Figure 1.3. Isaak and Sarina Saltiel with little Maurice. Archive of Eleni Saltiel.

His parents then approached a railway worker and gave him a monetary sum to transfer him to Larissa and then to Athens. He was dressed in the uniform of a railway worker and entered a train with Italian soldiers. He anxiously crossed the Tembi straights, where the Germans conducted controls, and arrived in Athens, which was then under Italian control. There he faced less danger. He was hidden with love and self-abnegation by Giannis Triantafyllidis (1923–2009) and Sotiris Faltsis (1922–2016).

He got a false ID under the name Sotiriadis. After a denunciation to the Gestapo that a family was hiding a Jew, the Germans conducted a search of the house where he was hosted. Maurice was able to escape. Maurice continued to hide, now at the home of Katina Kalogirou, the grandmother of Sotiris Faltsis, until October 1944, when the Germans departed. At one point, when the situation became harder, a trafficker promised that he could help him escape by boat to Egypt. However, on the day of the proposed escape, the trafficker disappeared, after receiving a big some of money.

In the meantime, his parents had been transferred to the ghetto next to the railway station in Thessaloniki. They were always supported by Maurice's friends, Giannis and Sotiris. This is the period when he corresponds with his mother. We do not know how many letters she sent him in total. Twenty-eight have survived. Sarina took with her the letters from Maurice.

Isaak and Sarina were deported with the fourth train on 23 March 1943 and arrived in Auschwitz five days later. Isaak was sick and sent directly to the gas chambers. No one from the family came back.

When the war was over, Maurice returned to Thessaloniki, traumatized forever over the tragic death of his family, who were all exterminated at Auschwitz.

He reopened his father's import shop, which he kept for many years. His main work, however, was his engagement with art in general, and with music in particular. Together with prominent personalities of the city, he founded the "'Techni' Macedonian Artistic Company," which was his vision and to which he dedicated a large part of his life.

In 1963, he married Eleni Nikolaou, and they had two children, Simos and Aris. He lived through yet another blow when his young son was killed in a car accident. Maurice died on 26 February 1998, four years after suffering a brain stroke.

In conclusion, I would like to thank wholeheartedly Leon Saltiel, who worked systematically on this edition, with kindness and calmness.

The part of this edition containing the letters from Sarina I dedicate to the beloved and invaluable friends whom I miss: Sotiris Faltsis, Giannis Triantafyllidis, and Vasilis Papamoschou.

Figure 1.4. From left: Sotiris Faltsis, Giannis Triantafyllidis, and Maurice Saltiel, standing, during a school holiday of the Second Boys High School of Thessaloniki. Archive of Eleni Saltiel.

Short Biography of Maurice Saltiel

Eleni Saltiel

Maurice, the only son of Sara and Isaak Saltiel, was born in Thessaloniki. He grew up in an urban environment with comfort and the love and affection of his mother, who played the piano, sang, and danced. He studied economics, but from a young age he fell in love with music and took violin, piano, and harmony lessons. He was interested in all the arts. He had very high goals and worked hard to realize them.

Consequently, in 1952, together with other intellectuals in the city, he founded the Macedonian Artistic Society "Techni" (Art), which was his main vision. In the years that followed, his artistic interests came to fruition. His initiatives and the consistent pressures and actions of "Techni" resulted in the creation of the State Orchestra of Thessaloniki and the State Theater of Northern Greece; the establishment of the Thessaloniki Film Festival; the development of activities in the visual arts, theater, and cinema; the organization of concerts and music competitions; and later the establishment of the School of Fine and Applied Arts in Thessaloniki. "Techni" developed collaborations with cultural associations throughout Northern Greece, which included exchanges of painting exhibitions, lectures, and recitals.

Maurice took the lead on ideas, but he was also actively involved in their implementation. He was a member of the board of directors of the State Theater of Northern Greece and the State Conservatory of Thessaloniki.

He greatly supported young, talented musicians with scholarships and any other means that he could offer. His main preoccupation was to promote artistic education. He wrote articles in the city's newspapers *Makedonia*, *Ellinikos Vorras*, and *Drasi*, always on cultural issues. He pointed out problems and offered solutions. He also wrote music reviews for the magazine of "Techni."

In conclusion, it is worth mentioning that he expended all his mental and physical strength for the artistic and cultural advancement of the city.

Architect and university professor Dimitris Fatouros wrote: "He was quiet, organized, persistent, ready to face difficulties, with reference always to music. He was not referring to himself, he was talking about others and art. A European intellectual."

Excerpts from the Autobiography of Maurice Saltiel

I am going to narrate to whom I owe my cultural education, and I am going to speak specifically about my mother, to whom I owe everything. The first musical instrument we acquired was a black German piano, standing straight, which was bought during the First International Fair of Thessaloniki, because my mother was playing the piano. After a while, they gifted me a small violin, and I started lessons with a Jewish violinist who used to play then in clubs and had his own orchestra . . .

Every now and then, my parents organized receptions that were often large, they invited an orchestra for dancing, there was a big buffet. My father reveled in life. My mother would stir up the friends with singing and dancing. An established holiday each year was my birthday on 31 May. I would then prepare a small piece on my violin, and I would perform to those assembled while my mother escorted me on the piano. After, I would read a small text that I had supposedly hidden in the case of the violin, which my parents had prepared promising that I would love the family and be a better child. Joy and pride in the family, congratulations from the guests, rich afternoon treats, sweets on a silver tray—there were two rare silver plates with two types of desserts, usually one type of homemade vanilla and one of bitter orange. There were also two silver cylinder containers for the clean and used spoons and, of course, glasses with water . . .

I continue with the celebration of my birthday. A milestone in the life of every male Jewish child is the coming of age when he enters or closes his thirteen years.

Figure 1.5. Maurice and Sarina Saltiel. Archive of Eleni Saltiel.

In this ceremony, which is called "bar mitzvah," the boy must know the portion of the Bible that is read on the Saturday of his birthday and take the position of the religious officer. They got me a teacher then who taught me the portion, because I also had to chant it.

In the books of the Bible, there are both the signs for the melody line and some dots for some vowels. The writing is from right to left, and the books are read from the back to the front. The parchment of the synagogue however does not have dots, so I had to learn it by heart. I remember vaguely only the first phrase with the melody line.

The day of the ceremony, the service took place, and in the afternoon we had a reception at home with rich treats. The next day, an evening reception took place. My parents' room was taken down, and they replaced the furniture with tables, an orchestra, and a big buffet. My mother wore a long gown, while I wore a tuxedo with short pants. Every birthday she took me and we would take a photograph of the two of us. The photo of that birthday with the tuxedo still exists . . .

In 1942, I came to Thessaloniki from Athens where I was studying for the summer holidays. My parents were already staying in an apartment with the grandparents and a family Marcos.

At one point, the Germans called all Jewish males to Liberty Square. It was the beginning of the end. Dad Faltsis had warned us that the German Commission in charge of the persecution was coming down to Greece. My father did not take it seriously. What he did was to slowly send merchandise to clients in Athens, in whom he had confidence.

We agreed immediately that I would escape to Athens. I went first via a small railway that takes you from Thessaloniki to Stavros in Halkidiki. From there, I continued on a mule until Neochori, Halkidiki, where I found my classmate Vassilis Papamoschou, who hosted me. He later became our pediatrician, and we are still close friends. From there, I was planning to take a caïque to go to the south, which was ruled by the Italians who did not persecute the Jews. Some people got suspicious of me, and Vassilis recommended that I return. I got back and learned the first news. Young Jews go to the "works" of the Germans. My father then paid a railway worker to take me toward Larissa. I got dressed as a railway worker and entered a military train with Italian soldiers. I had the cheekiness to start chatting with them, to speak in Franco-Italian about operas. It was to the great pleasure of the Italians. Anguish, however, for the Tempi crossing, where the Germans conducted checks. Eventually I arrived in Larissa and from there to Athens, and I went directly to the home of Faltsis. . .

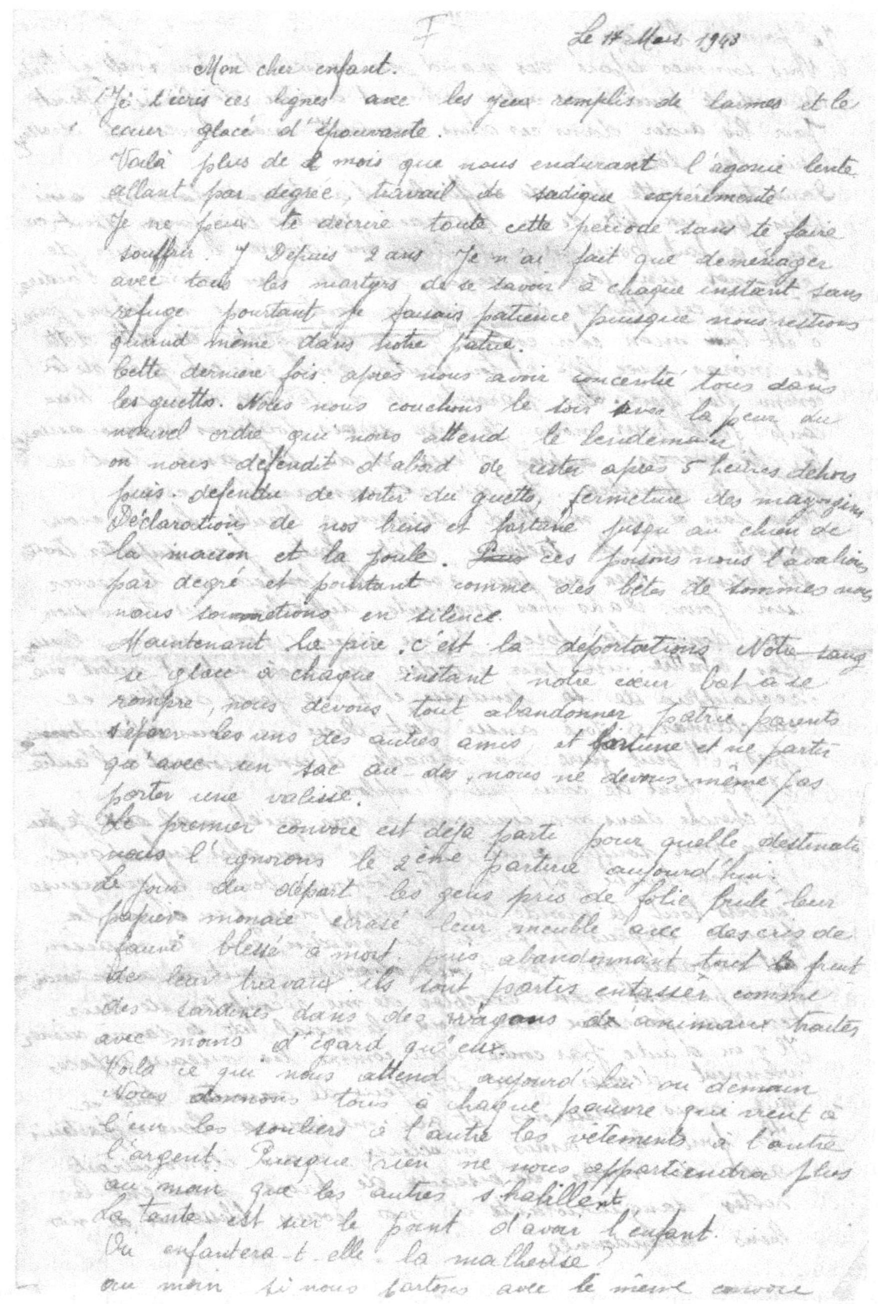

I

Le 17 Mars 1943

Mon cher enfant.

Je t'écris ces lignes avec les yeux remplis de larmes et le
cœur glacé d'épouvante.
Voilà plus de 2 mois que nous endurons l'agonie lente
allant par degrée, travail de sadique expérimenté
Je ne peux te décrire toute cette période sans te faire
souffrir. Depuis 2 ans je n'ai fait que déménager
avec tous les martyrs de se savoir à chaque instant sans
refuge pourtant je faisais patience puisque nous restions
quand même dans notre patrie.
Cette dernière fois après nous avoir concentré tous dans
les ghettos. Nous nous couchions le soir avec la peur du
nouvel ordre qui nous attend le lendemain
on nous défendit d'abord de rester après 5 heures dehors
puis défendu de sortir du ghetto, fermeture des magasins
Déclaration de nos biens et fortune jusqu'au chien de
la maison et la poule. Puis ces poisons nous l'avalions
par degré et pourtant comme des bêtes de sommes nous
nous soumettions en silence.
Maintenant le pire, c'est la déportation. Notre sang
se glace à chaque instant notre cœur bat à se
rompre, nous devons tout abandonner patrie parents
séparer les uns des autres amis et fortune et ne partir
qu'avec un sac au dos, nous ne devons même pas
porter une valise.
Le premier convoi est déjà parti pour quelle destination
nous l'ignorons le 2ème partira aujourd'hui.
Le jour du départ les gens pris de folie brûlé leur
papier monnaie écrasé leur meuble avec des cris de
fauve blessé à mort, puis abandonnant tout le fruit
de leur travail ils sont partis entasser comme
des sardines dans des wagons de animaux traités
avec moins d'égard qu'eux.
Voilà ce qui nous attend aujourd'hui ou demain
Nous donnons tous à chaque pauvre qui vient à
l'un les souliers à l'autre les vêtements à l'autre
l'argent. Puisque rien ne nous appartiendra plus
au moins que les autres s'habillent.
La tante est sur le point d'avoir l'enfant.
Où enfantera-t-elle la malheureuse?
ou moins si nous partons avec le même convoi

Figure 1.6. The first page of Sarina Saltiel's letter of 17 March 1943. Archive of Eleni Saltiel.

Letters from Sarina (Sara) Saltiel

Letter from Irene Marcos, 4 January 1942

My dear Maurice,

It's very kind of you to write to us, and it is with pleasure that I reply to your letter on behalf of my family.

Your parents have been with us for a month, and we spend every day together in the best possible way—thanks to your charming mother whom we all appreciate.

We are always altogether, even on the promenade, and we forget life's difficulties either by singing, exercising, or sitting calmly by the stove.

She thinks of you all the time, and it upsets her that you are far away; we console her by telling her that this is how one becomes "a man." It's during difficult times that we find out who we are.

I know you're preparing for your exams. I wish you the best of luck and success in your studies.

My family and my sisters, in particular, send you their greetings.

Best wishes,
Irene Marcos[1]

First Letter, 17 May 1942

My dear child,

I haven't heard from you for the past fifteen days. Thank God, I received your letter today from the 13th. I write to you almost every Sunday. I don't understand why you haven't heard from me. I already wrote to you, telling you that I received your two photos. I even gave you my opinion on the photographer.

I heard you're not eating well. Don't do that because you'll need the energy with the exams coming up. Make sure you eat healthy because I want to see you in a good condition when you return.

Father wants you to send him the medicine. Also send me ubrocarpine if you find some, because I suffer from arthritis, especially when it is windy.

I want you to buy me a little bit of fabric in a pretty pattern of your choice, and send it to me through Sotiris' mother,[2] or with the Greek guy that brought you the chocolates I sent you.

I hope you received the box I sent containing seven chocolate bars, two boxes of Gustav Porvolers, and some biscuits. Give one of the chocolate bars to Samy,[3] and two to Sigoura. The rest is for you. Do you want the swimsuit? I'll send it to you as soon as I can.

Today I went to a jazz concert performed by Michel Assael[4] and his orchestra. It was my first concert. It pleased me immensely. The venue was packed, and I met all of my old friends. I thought that you would come soon, too. The concert consisted of pasos dobles, tangos, and various other songs. The singer outdid himself, and Michel was overjoyed. I was so excited when I left that I went to the photographer to get my picture taken to send to you, but there wasn't enough light, so I returned home disappointed.

Once at home, I found that Uncle Jacque's family[5] had come over for dinner. I was invited to go to Aunt Sol's house.[6] They were having Samy's associate over for dinner. However, Father didn't want to go because he had taken a laxative. I really regretted not being able to go because I had wanted to get news of you through this gentleman.

I went to see a psychic yesterday to find out who stole my cheese. She told me two porters had stolen it. I then asked her when I would get my house. She replied that I would be given the key this week, but after much difficulty. Let's hope so.

The Marco ladies would have replied to you, but they've been very busy with their mother who has been sick for the past three weeks due to an abscess on her leg that got infected. I'm her doctor and her nurse, and they're very happy with the way I treat the wound. In the evening, I removed the pus—the most difficult part of the procedure—and I'm very happy to have succeeded. Hopefully, it will do for now.

I saw Manolis[7] yesterday. They all want to see you again.

Thank Samy for the stockings he sent me.

I hope the shoes fit you well. Change your socks every day so that the sweat doesn't give you a skin infection.

Give my regards to Sigoura, Samy, Sotiri, and his mother. Thank her for all the trouble she went through to give you the gift.

Your grandfather, grandmother, as well as your father send you their kisses. Everyone sends their greetings. Many loving kisses from your dear mother.

Sarina
I gave the invoice I found in your letter to father.

Second Letter, 26 May 1942

Dear Maurice,

I was surprised when you told me on the phone yesterday that you want to come back home without completing your studies. I don't know what to advise you. If you want to come back, make a decision after having weighed the pros and the cons. You'll always be welcome here.

Later, I was at father's store where we stored all the pieces of furniture the Kommandatur returned to us. They're in bad condition, but at least we got them back. Now we have to find a house. They kept everything, the curtains, the linoleum, the lamps, the bathroom, the telephone, etc. I hope to God that this is the last of our troubles.

I just received a letter from Samy, I'll reply to him as soon as possible.

I repeat, Maurice, for your return, do what you think is most reasonable. I know that you're quite capable of making a decision on your own.

Sotiri paid me a visit yesterday morning, and he gave me four boxes of shots, two boxes of passi-florine, and one bottle of urotropin. Jani[8] came to see me in the evening, but I'd gone to see father's cousin, Luna Ouziel, who has a daughter called Ninette whom you know.[9] Her husband died of galloping phthisis.

My regards to everyone. Kisses from me.
Sarina

Third Letter, 17 August 1942

My dear child,

I was very happy to read in your letter that you are in good health and in the company of Mrs. Kalogirou.[10] I'm not worried about you (ever) asking for her hand in marriage. On the contrary, I'm sure that you would be very well taken care of. I hope you'll be of great use to her, as she's all alone. You'll replace all her children. I know you're capable of loving her, too. Thank her on my behalf for the hospitality she has shown you.

Sotiri comes over often. I gave him four and a half pieces of silk like the one your shirt is made of. His uncle cut it up, and he'll be able to make two shirts out of it by adding another two pieces. They really appreciated it, and Miss Urania[11] told me that she found it to be a gift of royal proportions.

I won't forget to write to Vassili,[12] and to send him a silk dress for his sister. But make sure that you don't forget to write to him, as he's asked Janaki about you.

I gave a letter for you to Sotiri, I hope you received it.

Go to the Floca pastry shop on 4 Korai Street.[13] Ask for Mr. Nico Nicolaou, to whom I gave the parcel (containing one pair of pajamas, one undershirt, a pair of underwear, two shirts, three pairs of socks, and three handkerchiefs) through his friend, Mr. Attias. I'll try to send you anything else you may need as soon as possible.

I've fallen ill with diarrhea yet again. It's as if my intestines don't want to leave me in peace.

Albert Djivre left to work with another 600 people yesterday.[14] Ouziel has already been gone for fifteen days. Saby, Dona's husband, has become a street sweeper.[15]

I beg of you to start studying diligently, so that you pass your exams. Most importantly, make sure you study foreign languages, as they are necessary nowadays. Get rid of your laziness, and get back to work. Also make sure you have enough provisions to get through the winter. Don't do the same stupid thing you did last year. Buy yourself some coal to keep yourself warm.

If you give your blue-green jacket to the dry cleaners, make sure they don't ruin it.

Greetings from everyone and to everyone.

I embrace you fondly.

Your dearest,
Sarina

Fourth Letter, [25 August 1942]

My dear child,

I hope you received the two letters I wrote, along with the laundry package that I sent you through Nico Nicolaou.

Last Thursday, I sent you a suitcase, through Amariglio, containing: 1 raincoat—1 green suit—1 trench coat—1 green woolen cardigan—1 pair of white shoes—1 pair of rubber shoes—3 pairs of woolen socks—4 cotton pairs (dark)—2 more in white—7 shirts—1 flannel shirt—1 light blue flannel undershirt—7 pairs of pants—4 undershirts—2 pairs of pajamas—8 handkerchiefs—1 hat—1 pair of slippers—1 belt—1 pair of suspenders—1 utility knife—1 Elveta—1 white suit—1 black suit—1 gray jacket—1 swimsuit—8 scarves. You must check to see if this is correct.

You must have received the accompanying documents we sent you by now. The key is enclosed in this letter.

I heard you resumed your studies. I'll send you books as soon as I can.

I made a cheesecloth shirt for Janaki, similar to the one I would have made for you. I'm pleased with the way it turned out. As always, he brought a gift for your grandfather[16]—a carton of 300 cigarettes. We can't give him anything without him paying for it in one form or another. I invited him over for dinner tomorrow. He fills the house, it's as if you were here.

Mrs. Faltsis came over to see me yesterday, so that she can teach me how to make corn flour.

I went to see a house opposite the Lycée[17] today. It's old and in need of repair. We're fine with it. I hope the Kommandatur gives us the permit. I'll let you know if I get it.

I hope you are buying provisions for the winter.

I met Manoli. He told me that he would write to you soon. He still has a stomachache.

Grandfather, grandmother, father, uncle, and family send you their regards. Oli no longer visits us at home. She lives with her brother at their store now.

That's all for today, send my greetings to everybody.

Your mother,
Sarina

P.S. The key can't unlock the suitcase. Send it again to me by return mail.

Fifth Letter, [beginning of September 1942]

My dear Maurice,

I received your letter, and I'm happy to hear that you're well. I hope you received the suitcase. Regarding the pajamas, shirt, and stockings you didn't receive, they had been left here. I took them back.

I prepared your books, and at the first opportunity I get, I'll send them to you with the rest of the things.

I didn't see Janaki this week. I had him over for dinner last Saturday, and he brought me a present—a nice embroidery "metrito"[18] of very fine quality, and which was certainly very expensive. Undoubtedly, his mother made it for herself. As I had given him a shirt, he repaid for it immediately. It's impossible to do anything for him without him wanting to repay for it.

Saby and Jacques, Resie's husband, have gone to work.[19] We no longer have a man at Aunt Lea's house. Nini's husband underwent surgery for peritonitis. He'll also be leaving as soon as he gets better.

We went to see a house on Pavlos Melas Street today. It has three small bedrooms and a living room fit for dolls. It costs 525,000 drachmas, and it will be available in twenty days. I think we'll end up getting it since we can't find another house. Winter is coming. We cannot continue sleeping in the hallway.

Uncle Jacques and his family ate with us today. Elico's store is going well.[20] He's talented in sales.

The Marco family sends you their best wishes.

We took our first boat trip this morning. We took pictures, but they didn't turn out very well.

Give our regards to the Sigouras and to our friends, as well as to Mrs. Kalogirou.

I embrace you fondly.

Your dearest,
Sarina

Sixth Letter, 10 September 1942

My dear child,

It was with great joy that I read your letter dated 2 September. I hadn't received any news from you for fifteen days. I knew you were well thanks to Jani and Sotiri.

I gave Miss Irene your letter. It pleased her. She'll reply as soon as she finds the time because the wheat and tomatoes need a lot of tending to. They keep getting infested with insects. They have to be left out in the sun every day.

We haven't made any progress with the house we were supposed to get, as the current owner is no longer leaving for Albania on account of business. You can imagine how I feel without a house as winter approaches, and we are starting to outstay our welcome.

Pinhas had too many problems and is working now. His uncle will also begin working.[21]

Sotiri spent Sunday afternoon dancing. He really enjoyed himself. Mr. and Mrs. Faltsis spent the afternoon with us so as to leave Sotiri alone at home.

Yani came to see me. He told me he sent you six books, one notebook, and the "deltions"[22] through Diomidis Tsitsis.

I sent you a suitcase containing books, various photographs, a camera, new shoes, old shoes, a pair of military boots,[23] a coat, fabric for a new coat, a balaclava, a pair of gloves, a woolen vest, a suit vest, a wool scarf, a silk scarf, a robe, a leather bag, and a pair of pajamas. Father sent you the certificate. I'll send you the violin as soon as I can. I know more than you how much you value your dear companion.

I heard that you're staying with Mrs. Kalogiro. I'm happy to hear it, and I hope you'll continue to stay there after Sotiri arrives. He worked too much at the hospital today. He gave your father a second shot for typhus.

I hope you'll spend Saturday with the Segouras, and that you'll celebrate altogether.[24]

I want to write to Samy and Claire, but I've been so tired these days that I even put off writing you this letter. Give them our best wishes.

I would really have loved to be with you. Salonica has lost its charm now that you're gone, my darling, and I can no longer travel. Now I wish I could take a break.

The moment that you'll get your books, make sure you study hard so that you pass your exams—it would be a shame to fail the year.

Give my regards to Mrs. Kalogiro and thank her on my behalf for the care she provides you.

You have greetings from all of our relatives and friends. Your grandfather, grandmother, and your father send you kisses. I send you all my love and best wishes.

Sarina

Seventh Letter, 14 [September] 1942

My dear child,

I received your letter dated 30 August after receiving your letter dated 2 September, through Sotiri. It arrived on the night of the holiday. It's as if you had come yourself. It consoled me in your absence. I would have liked to have heard your blessings and to have blessed you during the prayers before dinner. Despite the distance between us, my heart is always with you.

I also lavish father with love. But it annoyed him that your maid found me beautiful. It flattered me, but I wish this compliment had been given to me by father. I would have valued it more.

I had Sotiri and Janaki over for dinner on Saturday. I always make them the best of what I have. They are always very happy.

I would have liked to use the telephone, but your father said it's for him.

Your letters are already a great comfort to me. I beg you though, my dear child, to write more clearly, as my vision is poor at the moment, and I have to spend a long time deciphering your writing. I think your mother deserves a little more effort.

And make sure you study French. Your letters are full of spelling mistakes and incorrect sentences. Your friends are learning better than you, and they spend less money. Sotiri speaks French well. Samico[25] is learning German. Nothing works for you. Now that I have sent you the books, study hard to make up for the lost time.

I saw Manoli on the street. He told me he also plans to leave for Athens.

Your father would like you to ask Samy for the accounts of the satin mousselinettes. What has he done with the money? Tell Samy to give you the amount that your father gave him, then call him[26] so he can tell you what to do with it.

Your grandmother's leg has healed completely, but she gets tired very easily. Your grandfather has also lost a lot of weight. He never rests either.

Your father isn't always in a good mood. Some days, he is so absorbed in his work that he doesn't even lift his head.

You asked me whether I felt anxious. Despite this anxiety, which is due to multiple reasons, I try to be in the best of spirts. I smile when I all I want to do is cry. I keep myself occupied and boost my morale as much as I can. I'm still living at your grandmother's place since I haven't found a house of my own.

I went over to find Samico's mother.[27] I didn't find her. I'll try again later.

That's all for today. Greetings to everyone from us. Your grandfather, grandmother, father, and your dear mother send you kisses.

Sarina
PS: I gave 3,000 drachmas to Gracien Nissim on behalf of Mrs. Elvira.
Sarina
PS: I've corrected a few of the sentences in your previous letter so that you write a bit better next time.[28]

My books, with s at the end
To give—after to, the verb give is in the infinitive
My boot-s, you need to put an s at the end of a noun when it is in plural form.
I will write to Sotiri and me "I will also write to Sotiri"
That I manage to keep it "That I have managed to keep"
The more best that I can "The best I can"
I goes out "I go out"

Letter from Irene Marcos, 20 September 1942

Dear Maurice,

I received your letter, and it was about time as we are all a bit upset with you. Especially Guita, after you left twice without saying goodbye to her; you'll have to write to her to make up for it.

The details of your living arrangements are interesting, and it seems that your life is well organized. I see that you don't waste time—that's good. Make sure you have fun, and take advantage of any distractions that may arise, but don't neglect your studies. It's also convenient to have your cousins nearby, and even though they can't replace your parents, they've offered you a home.

Your friend Sotiri comes over often, we chat with him sometimes. He has an alert and curious mind. He tries to understand everything, so he'll find his way in life. He's happy that you'll be together soon. He has a charming mother.

It's been 20 days since I last went to the beach, even though the temperature is mild. Notwithstanding, the weather has changed, and it upsets me greatly to see the summer coming to an end.

Together with our friends, we are part of a "group," and by strolling or staying at home, we try to spend our afternoons in the best way possible. Your dear mother is a part of this group.

I've resumed the studies I had previously neglected. I read a lot, and I'm very busy.

I'll happily answer your letters since you want me to.

I'd like to point out to you that your French isn't very correct. Pay attention to your spelling mistakes—a student shouldn't make such mistakes, and it isn't very polite toward those reading your writing.

Best wishes and greetings from my family.

Best regards,
Irene Marcos

Eighth Letter, 21 September 1942

My dear child,

I received your later dated 13 September, and I'm pleased to hear that everything is going well with Mrs. Kalogirou and her housekeeper. I visited Sotiri's mother who asked me for a bathrobe for you. Take a bedsheet or some white flannel—the only one we had was stolen from us when we moved house.

I'm writing to you from your grandmother's house again this evening. They have requisitioned the house, so I'm not sure where I'll be living tomorrow, nor does your grandmother and the Marco family. We're going to the Kuartiram[29] tomorrow morning to ask for another place to live. As soon as I have some news, I'll write to you.

I visited Samico's mother. She was deeply upset and crying. I believe that Sami spends every penny he earns instead of helping his family, which is currently going through difficulties. During my visit, some creditors came by to ask her for the money she owes them. I beg you to talk some sense into Samico who is intelligent enough to help a mother who sacrificed so much to bring him up and educate him.

And you, my dear Maurice, I hope that you're behaving yourself. Spend what you need to eat well, but don't let yourself be enticed[30] by certain young ladies who appear to be saints but are actually demons.

Today, I went to see Mrs. Faltsis whose leg hurts. We chatted about music and art. It made us both happy. I miss talking to you about these things.

I hope you received your books. Study as much as you can. It would be a pity for you to fail.

I wish you a happy holiday[31] and may my blessings and those of your father accompany you everywhere.

Send my best wishes to all of our relatives and friends. The old have become older. Father and I send you kisses and bless you.

Your dearest,
Sarina

Katina Kalogirou
21a Ithakis Street
Athens
For Mr. Saltiel[32]

Ninth Letter, [1 October 1942]

My dear child,

I apologize deeply for my delay in responding to you. I haven't been able to rest during the day or during the night for the past ten days.

As you know, our house was repossessed again. After many difficulties, we managed to get a house in the countryside[33] from the Quartiriam, located at the Constantinidis tram stop, Karaiscakis Street No. 5. It's a ground floor unit with three bedrooms: one for me, one for your grandmother, and the other one for half of the Marcos family because they only managed to get one room in the house we lived in. The move happened at 10 p.m. without electricity as the truck was only free at that time. Thank God that there was enough moonlight. I had to receive everything on my own. I almost died of fatigue.

In order to relax, we spent the night picking out bedbugs, slugs the size of fish, and mosquitos that have disfigured me and the entire family as well. There is no one here to help us. Only one helper at the store, as father is good for nothing. All of the work falls upon your grandfather and me. You should see how much weight your grandfather has lost.

Jani came to help me with the boxes in the other house. Instead of letting him help me, your father wanted to play tavli[34] with him.

Still, thank God we found this house. It's very close to the tram, and it's very beautiful. The only issue is that we can't leave the windows open. They are visible from the street, and easy to climb. We get used to anything now. This war taught us to be patient. Our new address is: Sarina Saltiel, Karaiscakis Street No. 5.

My company with Moise Fais[35] has been dissolved. Your Uncle Joseph remains his partner with a 25 percent share in the business. This upset me. They didn't consult me about any of this. They only sent me the document to sign.

Study hard so that you pass your exams and finish your studies quicker. That way, you'll be able to defend your interests. Everyone wants to take advantage of us, and father does things wrong.

I hope my next letter will be more pleasant. Give my regards to everyone.

Your grandparents, father, and mother send you a thousand kisses. I kiss you, especially.

Your dearest,
Sarina

Tenth Letter, 8 October 1942

My dear child,

Today I had the pleasure of seeing almost all of your close friends.

In the morning, I met Christos[36] walking shamelessly with that Tanda—the blonde dancer from Dalmaye[37]—and a friend of his. The lady was arm in arm with both of them. Imagine what this bitch must cost him. Too bad, he's losing himself more each day. I wouldn't be happy if I saw you in his company. May God always save you from falling into such hands.

In the afternoon, Mrs. Faltsis came over for a visit. I offered her a nice cream made of eggs and cookies. We chatted amiably. It is very pleasant to chat with her. Too bad we live far from each other.

She told me that her mother adores you[38] and that you want to buy a piano. Look my child, if you find a good secondhand piano, get it checked, and then buy it. But on one condition: that you promise me you'll learn to play it in earnest, and that you'll study harder. Don't leave things halfway like you usually do. You know that my greatest desire has always been to study music. It would make me very happy to see you make progress. I hope you keep your word. I spoke with father and he gave me permission for you to buy it.

Tonight I had Janaki over for supper. He played a game of cards with father. It makes both him and us happy to eat dinner together.

Pandeli[39] has been stuck at his place. His shoe hurt his foot, and as his mother is at her best woman's place,[40] Jani is taking care of him.

You haven't written back to tell me whether you received the straw suitcase. Let me know because we'll have to reclaim it otherwise.

We're starting to get used to our new home. The only problem is that there are too many mice—especially in grandmother's room. She insists on moving to another house, but we can't even find a free room.

The Marcos haven't moved to this house yet. But their room is ready. Mrs. Marcos came by this morning. She sees how good we are now and loves us even more. Me, too. I miss the ladies very much. Grandfather, who was used to teasing Margot, is now very bored because father is preoccupied with the store and doesn't talk to him.

That's all for now. Grandfather and grandmother keep asking about you. They embrace you fondly.

Greetings from the family of Uncle Jacques, as well as from all our relatives and friends.

Kisses from father and your dear mother.

Greetings to Samy and the Segouras.

Your dearest,
Sarina

[A new letter continues on the same paper]

My dear child,

While cleaning father's suit today (Sunday), I found your letter in his pocket. I blamed him for being neglectful. He didn't even respond after failing to run an errand for me.

I paid two visits to your friend Pandeli, who has hurt his foot. He's getting better. It gives me such a heartache to see sick children far from their parents.

I sent a brick-red silk dress to Vassili for his sister. I hope you're happy.

We've had uncle over with his family since the morning. Grandfather lit the stove today because it's cold, and we have to be ready for winter.

Janaki told me that you came in first in one of your lessons. Congratulations. Work in the office now, so you can buy the piano you wanted. Have fun and work. I work like a beast of burden from morning to night without ever receiving a word of kindness.

You seem very happy to be away. I console myself in your absence by thinking how, unlike me, you don't have to put up with father's foul character. I hope I'll be rewarded one day.

Many kisses,
Your mother

Eleventh Letter, 18 October 1942

My dear child,

I received your letter of 7 October with great joy. It consoles me during my moments of solitude.

I'm pleased with the exam results. I hope you pass the other three lessons, provided that you study well. From your letters, I gather you're not studying foreign languages. You'll regret it forever. For example, instead of saying "I gave iron my suit," we say, "I ironed my suit."[41] Later, when you'll have to write business letters, you'll see that you won't be allowed to make such mistakes. Next year, and God willing, you should receive your diploma, but your writing skills as well as your calligraphy are still very problematic. By hiring a teacher and with a bit of effort on your side, you can still improve these flaws.

The grandparents were very happy to read your letter. You should see how they took in every word I read. Oh, how I wish they didn't have to work anymore.

Grandfather is obliged to return on foot nearly every day at noon. It's impossible to take the tram. As for me, I rarely go downtown because I'd also have to return on foot.

We're getting used to this house. I've painted the kitchen, toilet, and the bathroom that we use as a storage room—our bath having remained in the old house. All our visitors congratulate us on our house, but it's thanks to my hard work of one month, day and night, that it's charming. The small things I have added, the way I have arranged it, and its cleanliness also make a big difference. No one helped me.

I had Costa Gourgou from Janitsa[42] over for five days this week with his wife and child. They have already left. Father went to Janitsa yesterday, and I'm alone.

It's midnight, and I can't sleep. I'm writing to you from my bed. This is the best way to converse with my son as there is no one to disturb me.

You told me you dreamt we were in Athens. May God fulfill your dream because there are times when my loneliness is so great that I wish I had wings to fly to you. Thank God you are well taken care of—this consoles me a little.

Thank Mrs. Kalogiro and her maid on my behalf for the care they give you. I'll try to send you the tomato paste as soon as I can.

Write to me about whether your new coat has been tailored, and be careful this time so that nobody steals it from you. We won't be able to replace it. Enjoy the new suit in good health.

I'm glad you're ok with Sami.

Now that you'll work and earn money, send a gift to the two good grandparents so that they may rejoice. They love you more than I do.

I had Jani over for supper this week. As soon as he arrives, father sits and plays cards with him. It makes us very happy when he comes because it's as if I'm taking care of you.

We have many visitors in this house because almost the entire family lives around here, and there is no staircase to climb.

The Marco family hasn't come by yet, and we're alone. I miss the ladies so much. I had things to talk about with them. I'd go out and forget about my troubles this way.

Albert Djivre has already returned,[43] but he has a fever. Almost everyone has a fever, and they're all very depressed. Mr. Eliezer Djivre, Albert's father, died at Demoticon.[44] Send a condolence letter to the Djivre family.

Give my regards to Elvire, and to the whole family. Likewise to Samy and all our friends. You have greetings from our relatives and friends. Kisses from grandfather, grandmother, and father. I embrace you fondly.

Your dear Mother,
Sarina

Twelfth Letter, 27 October 1942

My dear child,

I went to the cinema with Bertica ex-Haim on Friday to see the movie "Eternal Melodies"[45] by Mozart. They played the Mozart minuet that you always used to sing and play for me. This touched me enormously, and it made me feel nostalgic. How I long for the musical scores we played together.

I returned home and while sharing the details of the movie, I started to cry. Then grandfather gave me a letter from you, with what joy I read it. It was short, but at least it was from you and that consoled me a little.

Lidia stayed over for two days this week. I helped her make a coat. Irene will make a sports overcoat now. I'll help her, too. Has your new overcoat been made?

Janaki came to see me today. He told me his mother had a cold, and so did he. We have all started to get the flu. Make sure you don't catch a cold, either.

Soriti came on Wednesday. The Marcos ladies came as well. We chatted a bit.

Christos doesn't even return home in the evenings. It's sad to see how he's losing himself.

No one has returned from work except those who are sick. I've been told that Samuelico, our employee, is in terrible shape. Father has been taxed 4 million, uncle 4 ½, and Moise separately 1½.[46] May God see to it that this is the end of our misfortunes.

Uncle Joseph's Moses has jaundice. He must stay in bed for eight days.

Today, Elico told me to get you on the phone two days after you called him.

Today, father will try to get your card from the Town Hall, and we'll send it to you.

As of today, it's now been two years since our war began.[47] I hope that it ends now for everyone's sake.

I've sent you a box of caramels through Janaki's cousin, and Mrs. Triandafilidou[48] has sent you a carton of tomato sauce.

Father asks that you sell 50 dozen of Cosmidis' coils, which are with the Segouras. The latter also has some money that Cosmidis left them. Take it, and let us know how much it is.

We sent an amount of money to Samy last week from the store. Ask him what he did with it. Ask Samy for the receipt from the merchandise he sold, and which belonged to father. Inform him of the prices of the merchandise on the market.

Give my regards to Samy, the Segouras, Mrs. Kalogirou, and your maid, as well as to our old friends.

Grandfather, grandmother and father send you their kisses.

With all my love, your dearest,
Sarina

Thirteenth Letter, 1 November 1942

My dear child,

What a joy it was to hear your voice on the phone on Saturday. In my enthusiasm, I didn't know what to tell you. What a pity we were cut off at the best moment. Still, I'm happy.

I'll make sure I send everything you asked for. Regarding the soap, father told me that the Sigouras have 5 oka[49] of his soap in safekeeping for him. Take it, and when you hand over your laundry, make sure it's used sparingly because we can't find good quality soap anymore.

I received your letter of the 24th yesterday. Gloves—I would have started working on them but my back ached because of the move. I couldn't knit.

I was in pain every night in bed, and father didn't want to apply the suction cups on me. I told him, "If my Maurice had been here, he wouldn't have left me in this state." Sometimes I miss you so much. I hope we'll be reunited at the end of your studies.

Congratulations on your new suit and overcoat. I hope the Athenian tailor made you look chic.

I've sent you a box of caramels through Janaki's cousin and tomato cream through Mrs. Triantafilidou.

I made you quince marmalade. I'll try to give it to Sotiri. I already gave him the shaving brush, the black bag and the violin. I'll start working on your gloves soon.

Father is working on the issue of the permit to send you food. Let me know what else you need.

If you want to talk to father on the telephone, call the number 80-528 and say you're calling father. In other words—say the name of Isaac Saltiel, and give them the number they may reach you at.

Ask Samy again about the sales account of the satin mousseline.

I'm starting to make friends around here. I've already been befriended by the owner of the house and her daughter.

Bertica Haim always comes by to take me to the cinema. On Wednesday, the young Marco ladies spent the afternoon with me. You see, my dear child, even the young ladies seek my company. I've always sought your company, yet I am obliged to be far away from you, and you cannot enjoy my maternal love.

Give my regards to the Sigouras, Sami, Mr. Kalogirou, and your maid.

Uncle Jacques sends you his greetings. He was here yesterday with his family, but both Daizi and Oli left because they were feeling ill.

Grandfather, grandmother, and father send you their kisses.

A thousand kisses from your dearest,
Sarina
P.S. What did you do with Cosmidis' coils?
Mother

Mrs. Katina Kalogirou
21 Ithaca Street
Athens
For Mr. Saltiel

Fourteenth Letter, 26 November 1942

My dear child,

It's the second time that I've had to wait for four hours on the phone trying to reach you. I always get upset. Letters have also become very rare. I haven't received anything from you for fourteen days. I heard that you're also worried about not receiving any news from me, and yet not a week goes by without me writing to you.

As for me, I have too much work, nobody to help me—not even grandmother since she's at Aunt Lea's. She'll be back today. I'll have some company in the house at least. I can't even rest when I don't feel good because there is nobody to replace me and look after me. I feel your absence even more. I don't get any affection. As all mothers have been separated from their children, we have to make do without this luxury.

Let's hope you pass your exams so that you can finish your studies faster and be reunited with us. I'm glad Sotiri is with you. He's already like a brother to you—a loved one.

Jani never fails to come and see me. Pandelis leaves on Monday. I'll try to give him a few things for you. Vassili has already gone to his village.

The Marcos ladies never fail to come by and see us. It's their turn to sleep all six of them in a room. They miss us a lot because they don't have as a good time with their new neighbor as they did with me.

I'm starting to make friends in our new neighborhood, but I don't have time to go over to them so they come to my house.

Ninette Ouziel, our cousin, came over unexpectedly for dinner on Sunday. She always has something original to say. Father thinks she's amazing. As always, new people make an impression on him.

Irene Marco and Moses Nahmias' sister paid me a visit this evening. After chatting with her about various things, she told me she'd come see me more often because she liked me. She told me this without "intending to flatter me."

My favorite pastime is reading before I fall asleep at night, and reading all day. I send my thoughts to you as if you were present in everything I do.

I made leek meatballs[50] yesterday. They turned out so good that I told father how my Maurice would have eaten them with great delight.

Have you made any food provisions for yourself? Buy everything you can.

Today, grandfather worked hard to fix my stove, which was nearly falling apart. He's the carpenter, the electrician, the mason, etc., of the house, and he never receives a single word of thanks from father.

Give my regards to Sotiri, Mrs. Kalogirou, the maid, the Sigouras, Sami, and friends.

Greetings from grandmother, grandfather and father.

Many tender kisses.
Your dear mother,
Sarina

Fifteenth Letter, 2 December 1942

My dear child,

I finally received a letter from you dated 21 November. I was already worried. It was with great joy that I heard you on the phone on Sunday. The more I want to talk to you, the more I tend to be forgetful. Joy makes me lose my bearings.

You told me prices have dropped in Athens. Take advantage of this to buy food because it's very difficult to send anything from here at the moment.

Pandelis had promised to take a bag for you. Now that he's going to drive, he won't accept a thing.

Janaki just left from here. He dined with us tonight. Together with father, we talked about various matters. Father refused to accept our opinions. So I told Janaki, "See how much I miss Maurice, we understand each other."

I must also tell you that father is making progress in reading the newspaper and in geography. He always has the dictionary with him. He is better, calmer. I'm so happy he's doing well.

Elico is still sick. He has a temperature now and then.

On Sunday, we had a betrothal. Ninette Ouziel got engaged to Daniel Benveniste, a friend of Maurice Serrero.[51] He plans on becoming a doctor and is very competent. He has one more year of study in Italy. He's penniless at the moment. He'll work while living off Ninette's money. He has potential. Hopefully, he'll succeed and live happily with her.

We were present at the signing of the documents. After spending eight hours over there, we spent the evening at home discussing what they should do. His brother, Dino Ouziel, has become a decent fellow. I couldn't believe my eyes when I saw how conscientious and serious he's become. It's a pleasure to see such a transformation.

I've had a maid for the past two days, a walking skeleton. I'm exhausted, so I accepted to take her on. She was recommended by a friend of mine. When I first saw her, I was heartbroken to see the state she was in—skinny and with no hair. I refused to take her on. So she told me, Madam, take me until you find someone else. Because if I stay at home, I'll die of starvation. I took pity on her. She is starting to work slowly, but well. Father agreed. She goes to sleep in the evening. I'll make sure she eats well so she can recuperate and feel grateful.

Today, I found out that she had worked for Aunt Sol for a year. Her name is Esterina. She was with the Aunt when Samy was doing his military service. She knows you. She told me you would go there for dinner every Sunday. Samy must know her. It will be a little rest for me.

I have had a hen for the past three months. You should see how smart she is. At meal times, she goes up to the small kitchen window. She bangs on the window with her beak for me to open the door for her. As soon as I open it, she enters to eat dinner. She's an aristocrat. She only wants wheat or corn. If I chase her out without her having had enough to eat, she doesn't budge. If her stomach is full, she knocks on the door to leave.

Grandfather always goes to the store on foot. Grandmother is still getting older. What do you expect? Nobody stays young.

Give my best to Sotiri, his grandmother, and his maid. Give the Segouras and Samy my best regards. Father, as well as your dear mother, send you kisses.

Sarina

Tell Samy to buy an electric anti-horn razor with blades for Uncle Joseph from Sidoni Soel. If he doesn't find the razor, he must at least buy anti-horn razors so that Uncle Joseph can take care of his feet.

Sarina

Sixteenth Letter, 11 December 1942

My dear child,

I received your letter written on the 3rd with joy. It was with great sorrow that I learned of the death of Doctor Papas.[52] He was a great surgeon. I think of the pain Mrs. Kalogirou and Sotiri are going through and of the hopes and dreams they had for his future. Give them my condolences.

Father is mad at you and Samy over the reels. He says you let yourself get carried away by Samy, and that you've lost too much for a first business deal. He is particularly mad at you for not having informed him of your intentions beforehand. I try to calm him down as much as I can. I beg of you to inform us of how things go, so that you are in good standing. Don't give up hope if you lost. On the contrary, I am glad. It will be a lesson and a life experience. Think well before you act. Be wary of sweet-talking people who take advantage of your indecision for their benefit. I know you're smart enough not to repeat this blunder. As your confidante and your friend, answer me on this issue.

Our life here is always monotonous. We're all at home by 4:30. We have to go to bed early.

I went to Janaki's to get our wheat because it had been eaten by worms. I gave all of it to Uncle Jacques who is struggling to make ends meet.

On top of it all, Aunt Sarina is five months pregnant. That really takes the biscuit. Elico Saltiel is better. He gets up, but he's very weak.

The elderly are the same, as always. Grandfather always does all he can to fix the house. He is adding window frames at the moment. I love my father-in-law with all my heart.

Give my greetings to all. Grandfather, grandmother, and father send you their kisses.

A thousand kisses from your dear mother.

Sarina

Seventeenth Letter, 17 December 1942

My dear child,

I received your letter of the 9th together with your Cosmidis notes. Although you provide father with details on the reels, he insists that you consult him before making any major purchases.

What you need to do to be good between three old people, is that you must pamper each one so that they will be well looked after.

I saw Samico's father,[53] and he told me you were in good shape when he left. I hope this is, and will always be, the case.

I haven't seen Janaki for the past fifteen days. Things are difficult now due to transportation issues. I want to buy him something for his nameday.[54] Tell me what he would like and when he plans to celebrate it.

Irene Marco came over this morning. She's mad at you because you didn't reply to her letter. It's impolite of you.

Moise Nahmias' two sisters came over in the afternoon, and we spent the time chatting and knitting. It's cold now, and we can't go out often.

The dentist Maurice Molho pulled out two of my molars this week. I didn't feel any pain, thank God. I'm done with this rubbish, and I can take care of the others now.

Grandfather is alone again because grandmother is once more at Aunt Lea's. I try to keep him company as much as I can.

Now that you have a leave of absence, make sure you work hard and show father that, if you are capable of losing, you are also capable of winning. Also find a good French teacher. Make up for the lost time.

How are the Segouras and Samy? Give them my regards.

All of our friends and relatives send you their greetings.

Kisses from grandfather, grandmother, and father.

Tender kisses.

Your dear mother,
Sarina

Eighteenth Letter, 27 December 1942

My dear child,

We went to our cousin, Ninette Ouziel's, place last Sunday. We see each other often. Her fiancé gives father intravenous glucocalcium injections, which make him better.

We met two Italian officers there. We spoke in Italian about the different towns we had visited in Italy. Then I sang to them in their language. They left in good spirits.

On Monday, Jani took me to see "Iron Crown"[55] at the Apollo movie theater. It was very good. Then in the evening, he had supper with us. He treats us like a son, "may we never miss you."[56] He comes to see us once or twice per week, and I always make him stay for dinner.

During Christmas, I visited the landlady, whose name is Chrisoula, and her husband Manoli.

Manoli's fete was the following day.[57] So we went to visit him. He was very happy, especially his father and mother. He's grown fat again. Janaki had been due to arrive in the morning. It pleased me to see them all reunited once again. Janaki couldn't stop hugging Manoli. They were happy. Then all the friends came and they played cards. Only you and Sotiri were missing.

Manoli's grandmother was very pleased to make my acquaintance and asked me to send you her greetings. You can tell she loves you very much. Grandmothers always love you, just like they love me. Then her aunts, who came to visit and who know you, passed me their compliments.

I went over to the Marcos on Wednesday morning and received a warm welcome from them. I spent a nice day chatting, but in the evening I must have caught a draft. I have a stiff neck. It hurts every time I move my head. I've already massaged it, but it makes no difference.

Right now it's 3 after midnight. Before making a linseed compress, and so that you don't worry from the delay in writing to you, I'm writing to you from my bed. Father is preparing the milk coffee and the compress. I hope it will help because it's very annoying.

Today, Uncle Jacques and his entire family came over. Oli and Daisy graduated to the next grade and Elico stayed in the same grade. Write a letter to the children, so that they feel obliged to write back. It will please them. They are very nice now and are always writing poems for the day they will return home.

I read your letter to father like I always do. He persists in his opinions. You need to make a good impression on him so he calms down a bit.

Grandfather installed the stove in my room because it was very humid. He always works as hard as he can. He is my father and my friend. Grandmother is jealous because I prefer him, and when I speak well of him, she tells me that I'm not aware of his faults. Who doesn't have faults? Grandmother also works hard, especially when her grandchildren come by. She doesn't know what to give them anymore.

Give Sotiri, and your new family, my best wishes for a happy new year and thank them for taking care of you. Congratulations for making bread on your own.

Give my greetings to the Sigouras and Samy. Best regards from all us.

Grandfather, grandmother, father, and your dear mother embrace you fondly.

Sarina

Nineteenth Letter, 3 January 1943

My dear child,

The New Year has begun. I hope it will be better than the last one.

I haven't heard from you for the past fifteen days. Thank God, Aunt Sol, who spoke to you on the telephone, told me you were well. I hope the festivities—and nothing else—prevented you from thinking of me. Thank God, my torticollis has gone.

I don't have a maid, and I'm working a lot again. The woman I had hired had scabies all over her body and was rotten. She contaminated our house. I threw out everything she touched. That's what it's like to be pitiful. I took pity on her—kept her so that she wouldn't die of hunger—and in doing so, my house paid the price. Let's hope I find a replacement who'll help me forget her.

On New Year's Day, Salvator Varsano and father's cousins[58] came over with their husbands. After the men had finished playing cards, we sang and danced. Salvator's sister-in-law—Esther—sings very well and without any preparation. We had a nice time.

Today, we went with father to a concert in Titania given by artists belonging to a group from Salonika. It was more like a performance review. There were two beautiful ballet performances. It wasn't bad.

At the end of the concert, we went to see Mrs. Claire. It was Bertica's birthday. There were two babies. After the small ones had eaten, they made us stay.

In the afternoon, two little tellers sang and danced. After they left, I taught the Hungarian dance, along with some other dances, to Jouli, the Esthers, the Chimchis, and the Lezericos. While I was dancing with Lezerico, I told him how we used to dance together all the time even during working hours. Hopefully, we'll be able to have fun like this again.

Uncle Jacques' two daughters come by this week. Daizi would recite and sing a repertoire in bed in the morning and in the evening. This pleased father. They left this evening. As I wasn't home, grandmother let them leave. If I had been home, I wouldn't have let them leave because Uncle Jacques is suffering too much.

I didn't see Janaki this week. He's busy with his party, for sure.

I beg you, Maurice, to write me a long letter about your life. In this way, a part of me will be with you. I swear not a single moment passes without me talking to you as if you were by my side. I feel you close, yet so far away.

I don't have time to visit Mrs. Faltsis so we find comfort in the people we have over at the house nearly all the time. It's on the ground floor, so all passers-by enter. It's nice to have company, but sometimes we'd like to have a little freedom to make formal visits.

Irene Marcos slept over on Thursday evening. We had a nice time chatting in her company.

As soon as we woke up, we noticed that thieves had entered the courtyard and stolen a woolen blanket, two woolen jackets and pajamas that I had put out to dry (I had given them to the maid and then left them outside because of her scabies). Father immediately went to the police. I hope we get everything back.

Greetings to everyone. Kisses from grandfather, grandmother, and father.

Tender kisses, your dear mother.

Sarina

Twentieth Letter, 18 January 1943

My dear child,

I finally received a letter from you, it helped calm me down a little.

I see that you don't lack the company of family. Grandmother Kalogirou is a good housewife. She continues your education. I thank her.

You told me you made jam for Vassili. Is he in Athens? Did the Segouras congratulate you on your jam?

I'm also doing good things. I made filo pastry at home. I have people over nearly all the time, so I made a small baklava, little hand pies, and boudino,[59] which all turned out very good.

I took father to the movies this week. He felt so cold that he said he'd never set foot in another movie theater again—not even for a million.[60] You're lucky you have such beautiful theaters in Athens.

We went to the White Tower theater yesterday morning. In addition to not having any stage props or costumes, the things they said were so unsettling that we felt nauseous. Having spent 2000 drachmas on the tickets, we left in disgust.

We celebrated the marriage of Miss Perahia, the banker daughter's, at midday yesterday.[61] You've met her, she's the youngest child who used to go to grandmother's neighbor. She was a charming bride, and there were distinguished guests at the wedding. It was quite the event—with well-dressed people wearing hats. We're no longer used to seeing such chic people.

After the wedding, we went home with Salvator Varsano's family and the parents. We spent the evening together and sang.

The Marcos ladies come by often to see me. You are the rudest person in the world to have left a young lady unanswered. I see that school doesn't teach one manners.

Father is still angry at you about the coils. Making a good transaction will help him change his mind about you. You know him—he's stubborn. His nerves are better. From time to time, he suffers from minor crises, which I patiently put up with.

Uncle Jacques didn't come by yesterday, as he does every Sunday, because Elico was sick.

Grandfather is very bored—besides going back and forth to the store on foot in the morning, he doesn't leave the house in the afternoons because the café isn't heated. I don't know how many times I refrain from going out, so as not to not leave the old people alone. My friends come over and we spend our time chatting.

Give my regards to the Sigouras and to Jani. Tell him that it was a pleasure to have spoken with him on the phone. He's still quite the comedian. I hope you two cousins are still getting along.

My greetings to Sotiri and his family.

Grandfather, grandmother, and father kiss you tenderly, and your dear mamica sends you kisses.

Sarina

Twenty-First Letter, 26 January 1943

My dear child,

Why are you too lazy to send news of yourself to the only person who waits impatiently for it? Write to me often. I feel you are next to me when I hold one of your letters in my hands. At the very least, don't deprive me of this sweet illusion. I wasn't fortunate enough to have my daughter to fill the void of your absence during your studies. Don't make me regret it more. Write down what you're thinking about, what you're doing. That way—it would feel like we were close to each another.

I'll give you an account of my daily activities, so that you are aware of what I do.

It was with joy that I heard your voice on the phone on Sunday, but the call was ended after a few words. I went home in anger. It was good the weather was nice. Our friends came over. We took a walk across the fields. It calmed me down somewhat.

Last Tuesday, I went to get the wood we had left at our house in Patron Germanos.[62] It was completely empty. They said thieves had taken it. I'm certain that the owner is the thief because he behaved in the worst possible manner toward me. Not a week goes by without us having some sort of trouble.

Janaki came by in the evening. I made him stay for dinner. He's the only one who replaces you here.

Elico is fine. I have him stay at home so that I can nourish him. This way, he can recuperate a little. I make him exercise every day so that his chest improves.

On Thursday, I had the Chimchis, Marcos Nahmias, and Ninette over with their handiwork. We chatted. Then we sang and danced. We have fun as a family now.

I'm going to get my teeth fixed. They have asked for 1,200,000 drachmas. I put off paying it every day, but I think I'll make a decision this week.

Last night, I had Costa Gourgoula from Janitsa stay over. I think he'll stay today, too. Father is wonderful when we have people over.

Everything was covered with snow when we woke up this morning. It's the first time. It's beautiful, but not good for those who have to walk and for those who lack comfort.

Mrs. Esther Naar gave me a letter from Cheli addressed to you so that you buy some books for her. I told her to speak to Manoli, and I'm waiting for an answer from her. He might have them. If not, I'll send you the letter and you can try to find them.

I'll stop writing for today, but I won't send my letter yet in the hope that the postman delivers one from you around 11 o'clock.

[In a different colored ink] As I predicted, the postman handed me a letter dated the 17th from you at 11 o'clock. I gave him a 50 drachmas tip. He really deserved it because it's freezing cold. As no one had gone to the office, I sat and read it to them right away. The letter made me very happy, and I reread it several times. Grandmother made me read it again saying that she couldn't understand it very well.

Bravo. You do everything yourself. Just as I had predicted. See how important it is to know everything? I wanted to teach you everything when you were with me. I see that Sotiri is also capable of everything.

You all turned out very well in the photos. The girl is very nice. She's as fat as you. This might mean she has a nice personality.

It is -5 and snowing today. It's also sunny.

Yesterday Bertha Haim took me to the movies. Grandmother wouldn't let me leave in the snow. We left anyway and took Elico with us as well. It was beautiful outside in the snow. We saw the movie "Abbandono."[63] It wasn't bad. Berthe asked me to tell you not to forget her.

Oro sends his greetings. She's more talkative than she used to be. There's nothing better to be done on this.

Grandfather, grandmother, and father send you their kisses. Greetings from all to all.

Tenderly yours,

Your dear mamica,
Sarina

Twenty-Second Letter, 1 February 1943

Dear Maurice,

The weather has changed. We're starting to get some sun. On Saturday morning, I took advantage to walk across the fields in the snow.

This week I had Buenica, the dressmaker, come over to fix some old clothes. We're not making anything new now.

Elico is spending the week with us, and he comes in to see what we're doing all the time. He prepares the food. This reminds me of my Maurice, who loved to help me when I was busy.

Ninette invited me at midday on Saturday to her place together with her friends. I made her cake. In terms of cleaning, she's useless. I was the only lady, and yet it was I who kept them entertained. The other girls invited me to their homes as well.

Now, Maurice, we need to see to Ninette's future fiancé. He's a good guy who was offered a scholarship to study at the Italian school. The latter sent him to study medicine at the University of Padua in Italy. He was a brilliant student there, too. They knew he would become a competent professor, so they even offered him a teaching post at the university. Unfortunately, the war interrupted his studies. He wants to continue them in Athens now, but he can't afford it. He wants to work as an intern in a hospital or clinic while continuing his studies. For this reason, you'll find a letter addressed to Doctor Karapiperis, 42 Solomon Street, enclosed hereto. I don't know if the address is correct—you've already been there once so you'll be able to find the house again. I'm asking him whether he can do something for Daniel. Ask him in person and mention that he would be helping a very talented future doctor find a position. He's quite a decent person so we might succeed with a little good will. Once you get the letter, give it to him and reply to me as soon as you can so that I see how he welcomed you.

Also ask Sotiri if he can help him find a position on his side. We must do everything possible so that he can graduate and practice. He's only missing three months of studies.

Uncle Jacques and his family send you their regards. Grandfather, grandmother, father, as well as your dear mother, kiss you.

Write back quickly. A thousand kisses from your dearest.

Sarina

To present the letter to Doctor Karapiperis, put it in a clean envelope.

Twenty-Third Letter, 8 February 1943

My dear child,

In your letter of 24 January, you tell me you've started playing your violin again. It's good, but don't do that "donkey race" where you run in place, like you always do. This sort of expression is allowed between a mother and her son. If you had listened to me, you would have been a virtuoso today. Your laziness always held you back. First and foremost, you need to get a calligraphy and spelling teacher. We can't decipher your scrawl like pharmacists can.

I give French lessons to Elico who remains at home. He takes advantage of it. He loves me a lot, and helps me when I have work.

Today I had pain in the liver. I had to remain in bed. He took care of me, just like you used to when I was sick.

Oro is missing. Her daughter was supposed to get married.

I no longer feel any pain, and I'm writing to you at 10 o'clock at night because I don't feel sleepy.

I have a lot of news for you this week. I'm currently looking after Mr. Modiano from the Modiano pastry shop. He has a staphylococcus on his back. Half of his back was infected. He asked me to treat him because I had once healed him and his sister of a purulent abscess. I began right away. I became a surgeon. I opened up the wounds with a razor blade. I removed a ton of pus after the operation, and sent him to sleep. He came back in the evening for me to change his bandages, and he was delighted because he was able to sleep and he no longer felt any pain. I continue to think about it.

The wound improves day by day, but father, having seen the courage I needed to treat the wound, would leave in order to avoid looking. He told me not to treat anyone else, because he doesn't want sick people coming to the house. When this gentleman heals completely, I'll feel proud to have done an excellent job.

On Wednesday, we were invited to Salvator Varsano's house. The gentlemen played first. The ladies and I chatted about many things and then talked about literature and recited beautiful poems. Around 5 o'clock, the men ended their games. We sang, danced and laughed until we cried just like we did before the war. The hallway was very wide. We were at ease.

On Friday, Janaki and Vassili came by to take me to the movies. We went to see "Viennese Blood."[64] It was superb. Full of beauty, joy, and music. There was no tram when we left. We returned on foot. Accompanied by Jani, Vassili sang charming little songs. He has a nice voice.

We had dinner together when we got back. In place of you, we had your photo. Vassili was more eloquent than ever. I'll be happy to be able to give him something for you when he leaves.

On Saturday, it was Benis Naar's[65] Bar Mitzvah.[66] We only received visitors, we'll celebrate it after the war. I gave him a shirt as a present.

Both Esthers are still angry. Neither Juli nor Rita came to give their wishes.

Enclosed, you will find a letter from Cheli for you to buy her books.

I stayed in bed today and Varsano, his family as well as his beautiful sister-in-law and brother-in-law, came over and took turns telling me short funny stories or singing songs on my bed. Uncle Moses Abravanel came, too. He is unemployed and doesn't even have a store.

I hope you've completed your mission with Doctor Karapiperi, and that you've received a favorable response.

Uncle Jacques and his family didn't come today because Oli was unwell.

I won't wait for the mail, so as not to keep you waiting.

Greetings from everyone. Grandfather, grandmother, and father send you their kisses.

Tender kisses from your dearest,
Sarina

Twenty-Fourth Letter, 9 February 1943

My dear child,

In my last letter, I spoke to you at length about Mr. Daniel Benveniste, the fiancé of our cousin Ninette Ouziel. He'll introduce himself to you. Please welcome him and help him out. Introduce him to the Segouras. Mr. Haim, who is acquainted with the Cannettis, may be of use to him.

Sotiri could help him get admitted to the University and, if possible, help him enter a hospital or clinic as an intern. I've made you his representative. May your house welcome him as his house welcomes you.

I kiss you tenderly.

Your mother Sarina.

Twenty-Fifth Letter, 23 February 1943

My dear child,

I apologize for the delay in responding to your letter. I was so busy and tired.

I've settled into the bedroom of our house at 43 Ptolemy Street now.[67] I opened up a door on the side of Mr. Ruclas' place. We still have a neighbor in our kitchen. The room is big, and I arranged it as comfortably as I could.

Cloui Djivre,[68] the Chimchi girls, and the widow Tamar—a cousin of Aunt Sol—moved to Aunt Sol's. Grandfather and grandmother moved to their house on Mizrahi Street.

Janaki helped me a lot. Please show gratitude toward him, always. He's like a son to me. Madame Faltsis came to visit me. She was also very kind. I thank them from the bottom of my heart. The Nahmias sisters also helped me.

I hope Mr. Daniel has been approved by Dr. Karapiperi, and that he's started studying. Give him my regards and tell him that Ninette came to visit me, and that she's doing well.

Was the concert at the Polytechnic School successful?

The Sigouras must be cramped in the house. Give them my regards and thank them for the warm welcome they gave Mr. Benveniste.

I'm in father's office right now. I think I'll come here every day since it's near the house.

Daisica sleeps with me every evening. She likes me and is like a hot water bottle in bed. Elico helped me a lot these days, but he's had the measles for the past two days.

Give my regards to everyone. Write to us more often. I'll write to you at length in my next letter.

Father and I send you tender kisses.

Your dear mother,
Sarina

Twenty-Sixth Letter, [beginning of March] 1943

My dear child,

Don't worry about not hearing from us. We can't communicate any longer. We're trapped in ghettos. We can't communicate with our relatives from the countryside.[69]

All I can say is that we're going through a critical period. We only have hope in God. One hopes not to lose reason. I try to be patient and philosophical about it as much as I can. We have all declared our assets and fortunes.[70] Our stores are closed.

Always be grateful toward your two friends, please. They have shown themselves to be worthy. Kiss your cousins on our behalf and give them courage.

Don't stay outside for too long so as not to catch cold.

Father and I send you tender kisses.

Your mother,
Sarina

If you ever need anything, your two friends will help you.

Twenty-Seventh Letter, 17 March 1943

My dear child,

As I write these lines to you, my eyes are filled with tears and my heart is filled with ice-cold terror.

We've been going through agony that has gradually increased these past two months—the workings of an experienced sadist. I can't describe what we're going through during this time without upsetting you. For two years, all I did was move apartments, conscious of the fact that we could end up homeless any moment; nevertheless, I was patient because at least we were allowed to remain in our homeland.

This last time, having being moved into the ghettos, we go to bed at night fearing the new order that awaits us the next day.

We were first forbidden to stay outside after 5 o'clock. Then, leaving the ghetto was forbidden, stores were closed, and we had to declare our assets and fortune—to the family dog and the chicken. We swallowed this poison gradually and, like the beasts of burden that we are, we submitted in silence.

The worst now is deportation. Our blood runs cold at all times. Our hearts beat to the point of bursting, we must abandon everything, country, parents. We'll be separated from each other, from friends and fortune, and we'll have to leave with a backpack only. We're not even allowed to carry a suitcase.

The first convoy has already left.[71] We don't know where to. The second one will leave today. On the day of departure, people go crazy; they burn their paper money, destroy their furniture with the cries of mortally wounded animals. Then, after abandoning all the fruits of their labor, they leave packed like sardines and treated worse than animals in cattle wagons.

This is what awaits us either today or tomorrow. We give everything to any poor person that comes along, shoes to one person, clothes to another, and money to yet another. Since nothing belongs to us anymore, we might as well clothe others.

Aunt is about to give birth. Where will this poor girl give birth? If we were to leave on the same train, I would be able to help her at least.

We've been separated from grandfather, grandmother, and from your aunt and uncle. When I think of these old people with none of their children around to help them during these hard times, the hairs on the back of my head stand up.

Your friend was more than a son to me during this difficult period. I'll never be able to repay him for everything he did for us. I'll be a mother to him should God grant me the power to return one day. I'll help him with his studies. If I'm not allowed to, you my dear child, must clear this debt. You must live with him and the other friend of yours[72] like brothers. His parents have also done a lot for us. I'll always be grateful to them. With them, you'll find everything you need. I recommended you to them.

I don't know what awaits me tomorrow at dawn. If we also get deported, I'll try to be strong and endure all the pain just to be able to see you again one day. May the vision of you give me strength during these difficult moments. I'll say to myself, "No, we'll never give up. The day will come when my beloved child will warm me with his love and make me forget this nightmare." Be just as strong. God won't abandon us. God can perform a miracle any time. There are so many hearts imploring him.

I try to think of what I could have done wrong to deserve such suffering. I swear to you my dear child that I can't find any reason. I've always been kind and generous to everyone. I received proof of this these last few days. Since 7 o'clock this morning, the house is full of friends; everyone wants to help me, but the only thing they can do is surround me with their affection. At least it makes you feel better to know you're loved.

However, there are others who, like birds of prey, come to devour what we leave behind, and which could not be theirs, with covetous eyes. These people are sweet-talking friends who wish to grab the bloody remains of our wounded hearts and abandoned property with the nails of birds of prey.

Father doesn't know what to do. He comes and goes. He can't help me in any way, so I have to think of everything. It's as if I had a child, and I treat him like one. May God give me strength enough for two so that you may see him again.

He sends you his blessing along with mine. May God always protect you. Be good and generous with everyone. Beware of sweet-talkers because they always keep their thoughts hidden.

Love your cousins like you love your brothers. May no discord ever separate you. Thank all the friends and parents you have over there on my behalf.

I'll leave you now, my dear boy, I kiss you and pray to God for a miracle tomorrow, so that I can write another joyful letter to you and even bless our enemies.

Father sends you kisses. I cover you with tender kisses.

Your friend, your dearest, your mother.

Twenty-Eighth Letter, 21 March 1943

My dear child,

What else can I tell you besides the slow agony we're going through? Three trains have already left filled with the unimaginable suffering of people who are penniless, who have nothing—only a backpack. Those of us who are still here are dying every minute from a rush of so many emotions. We've tried everything, but we haven't achieved anything.

This might be the last letter I write to you. I bless you. May the Lord keep you.

You'll never be able to repay your friend for what he's done for us. You must be more than a brother to him. You owe your life to him and to the other friend of yours who is by your side.

If the Lord grants me the joy of seeing you again one day, I wouldn't know how to bow down before him.

Father is completely discouraged. I support him with the little courage I have left.

I'm leaving you my beloved child, and send you tender kisses.

My heart is broken.
Sarina

Letter from Zak Serrero, [beginning April 1943]

Dear Maurice,

On the occasion of the departure of our common friend, I write you below our situation here at great length.

Following the sad decision of the occupation authorities to persecute the Jews here, almost three-quarters of the population have been sent in an unknown direction. The young men are separated from their families and are sent for labor. Their parents remain here for now.

Unfortunately, they do not allow anything to be taken with them, not even money, apart from the necessary things that one can carry by oneself.

The deportation, if we want to name this persecution, happens as follows:

Around 5 a.m., they surround an area without prior notice, they give half an hour deadline to get ready. Sick, small children, elderly are carried to the Baron Hirsch neighborhood (train station stop). There, they gather, stay for approximately 3–4 days, and are sent to an unknown direction, they say it is for Poland.

Unfortunately, with sadness I let you know that your father and mother were sent yesterday.

Grandfather and grandmother still remain here, they were not able to kiss them though. I remain because, on the day of the rounding-up, a daughter was born.[73] We named her Lily (Lea), the name of the grandmother's sister who died recently. I don't know how long I will stay here. Maybe this is my last letter.

A great robbery has taken place for the merchandise of the shops and the furniture of the homes. When the owners depart, German cars come and collect all the items that are located inside the homes.

Our situation is tragic. We cannot go out of our homes without permission and without the escort of a civilian guard. The day before yesterday I was able to see my parents with the pretext that I went to register my daughter at the registry office.

Father left money and items to the people that you know, and this is for your knowledge, in case you need one day.

With tears in my eyes I close this letter. Maybe it is my last letter, I don't know if we will see each other. If after the war God would like us to survive, write to the Red Cross in Geneva, Croix Rouge Internationale à Genève, so we can meet.

I kiss you with Aunt Sarina and my children.

Z. Serrero[74]

Notes

1. Haim and Buena Marcos had four daughters: Irene, Margo, Lydia, and Lelia, all victims of the Holocaust.
2. Ms. Ourania Faltsi, mother of Soriti, Maurice's classmate.
3. First cousin of Maurice, who lived in Athens.
4. Michel Assael had studied music at the State Conservatory of Thessaloniki during 1934–37. He was deported to Auschwitz and survived as a member of the camp's male orchestra. After the war, he migrated to the United States.
5. Zak Serrero, Sarina Saltiel's brother and Maurice's uncle. His wife was also called Sarina. He had four children, Elias (born 12 July 1930), Sol (10 March 1932), Daisy (1935), and Lea (3 April 1943). They were all killed in Auschwitz.
6. Wife of Joseph Saltiel, Isaak's Saltiel brother and Maurice's uncle.
7. Maurice's classmate.
8. Giannis Triantafyllidis, Maurice's classmate. Also referred to with the diminutive "Janaki."
9. Luna Ouziel, née Carasso, had three children, Dinos, Ninette, and Polin, who all survived.
10. Katina Kalogirou was Sotiris Faltsis' grandmother. Her family originated in Alexandria, they owned tanneries in Chios Island, and she was born in Istanbul. Her home was in the Kipseli district of Athens. Her name is often written in the letters with Greek characters.
11. Sotiris Faltsis' mother.
12. Maurice's classmate.
13. This was the first shop of the known Floca patisserie in Athens. The address is written in Greek.
14. For forced labor. Albert Djivre of Elizer was born in 1903. His wife was Clara Chimchi (Simsi) and stayed at 2 Misrahi Street. He was deported and killed in Auschwitz.
15. A group of 230 Jews, conscripted for forced labor, were given to the cleaning service of the Municipality of Thessaloniki by the German occupation authorities. Saby refers to Sabetai Roubissa, who was working for the Municipality and fired on 6 March 1943. He was born in 1899, his wife was called Dona, and they had three children, all victims of the Holocaust. His property declaration has survived, which lists his profession as "municipal street sweeper."
16. She refers to her father-in-law, who stayed with his wife at their home.

17. The French Institute of Thessaloniki, an institution that exists in the same location today.
18. A Greek word in Latin script meaning “counted”; a type of embroidery.
19. Forced labor.
20. Eliau, son of Joseph Saltiel, born in 1922.
21. Forced labor.
22. Greek work for the ticket for the daily ration.
23. Uses the Greek word *arvilas*.
24. Rosh Hashanah, the Jewish New Year. In 1942, the eve was on 11 September.
25. Sam Saltiel was Maurice’s first cousin.
26. She used a Greek expression, translated to French.
27. She refers to Sam’s mother, Sol Serrero, who was married to Joseph Saltiel, brother of Sarina’s Saltiel husband. Even though the two women had the same last name—Serrero—they were not related. The couple had four children: Moise, Sami, Eliau, and Isaak. All survived.
28. She is correcting her son’s French.
29. Quartieramt, the German district office.
30. She is using the Greek word *coroydes* in Latin script, which means “fool.”
31. The holiday of Yom Kippour, the Day of Atonement, which started on 20 September 1942.
32. Address written in Greek script.
33. This is the name of an old district of Thessaloniki, today along Vassilissis Olgas avenue.
34. Backgammon.
35. Moise Fais, of Solomon and Lea, was born in 1898. His wife was called Palomba-Nelly née Beniamin, and their son was called Samuel. Their address was Patron 21, and he was a shopkeeper. Moise Fais was deported and died in Auschwitz, bearing camp registration number 115035.
36. Friend of Maurice, with his name changed.
37. Tanta Valic was an actress, singer, and dancer who participated in several productions in Thessaloniki during the Second World War. After the war, she was accused of collaboration with the Germans but the charges were eventually dropped.
38. Ms. Kalogirou.
39. Maurice’s classmate, Peandelis Petroutsopoulos.
40. She used the Greek word *coumbara* in Latin script.
41. She is teaching him the correct phrase in French.
42. The Greek town of Giannitsa, some fifty kilometers from Thessaloniki.
43. From forced labor.
44. The Greek town of Didymoteicho, near the Greek-Turkish border.
45. An Italian historical drama produced in 1940.
46. It refers to the ransom that the Jews of Thessaloniki were obliged to pay for the release of the forced laborers.
47. She refers to the rejection of Italian dictator Benito Mussolini’s ultimatum by Greek Prime Minister Ioannis Metaxas, on 28 October 1940, which entered Greece in the Second World War in the side of the Allies.
48. Giannis’ mother.
49. An Ottoman measure of mass, around 1.3 kilograms.
50. This is a traditional Sephardic recipe.
51. Ninette got married to Benveniste in the end. In 1946, Benveniste was a doctor in Athens. Maurice Serrero of Sabetai also survived and after the war immigrated to Israel.
52. Alekos Pappas was an urologist, relative of Sotiris Faltsis.

53. Joseph Saltiel, Maurice's uncle.
54. Saint John's day, celebrated on 7 January each year.
55. Italian adventure film produced in 1941.
56. Phrase written in Judeo-Spanish.
57. Manoli celebrates on 26 December each year.
58. Salvator Varsano, with this wife Clara Sadikario and her sister Ester. Varsano survived the war.
59. A type of cake.
60. The weather those days was exceptionally cold.
61. Germaine Perahia was the daughter of Jeshua Perahia, director of the Union Bank. She got married to Leon Cohen on 17 January 1943. Jeshua Perahia became President of the Jewish Community of Thessaloniki, from 1949 to 1954.
62. Paleon Patron Germanos Street, in the center of Thessaloniki.
63. An Italian historical drama produced in 1940.
64. A German operetta film produced in 1942.
65. Benis (Benjamin) Naar was born on 8 February 1930. He and his parents, Solomon and Ester, were victims of the Holocaust.
66. Jewish ceremony for the coming of age for boys.
67. Forced to move to the ghetto.
68. The wife of Albert Djivre, Clara Chimchi.
69. The name of a district of Thessaloniki, east of the city center.
70. The declaration of fortunes was mandated on 1 March 1943.
71. The first train departed on 15 March 1943.
72. She refers to two friends, schoolmates, and university classmates of Maurice, Giannis Triantafyllidis, an architect/urban planner and professor of the Polytechnic School, and Sotiris Faltsis, a doctor.
73. She was born on 3 April 1943.
74. Brother of Maurice's mother, letter written in Greek.

Part II

Barouh Letters

Introduction

Leon Saltiel

Mathilde Barouh exchanged letters with her son Fredy, who was located in Athens during the war. The eleven letters that have survived cover the period from 28 February to 17 April 1943. Her last address was Amalias 30–32, in the large ghetto in the east of the city.

Ms. Barouh was born in 1883, and her address was Georgiou Nikolaidou 17 in Thessaloniki. Her family name was Kamhi, and she originated from Monastir, today Bitola. Her husband was Maurice (Moses) Barouh; he was from the city of Ioannina and was a fabrics merchant. He passed away in 1916 in Istanbul due to the Spanish flu. At the time, the family lived in Istanbul, but they returned to Thessaloniki, where they had relatives.

Fredy (Alfred) Barouh was born in Thessaloniki in February 1915. During the war, he lived with Annette Calderon in Athens, who was a cousin of Mathilde. According to his son, Morris, Fredy—presumably after the Italian capitulation in September 1943—escaped to the Middle East and enlisted in the Allied forces. He served as an interpreter in the Second Division of the Greek army there and took part in the Allied debarkation in Rimini, in September 1944, where Greek forces also participated. After the war, he worked in the trading of fabrics, and later timber.

He got married to Yola Barouh, née Mourtzoukou, from Volos, who came from a prominent family of industrialists. It was she who donated the letters to the Jewish Museum of Greece. Fredy Barouh passed away on 19 May 1973. The couple had one son, who lives in Athens with his family.

Figure 2.1. Mathilde Barouh in her wedding dress. Archive of Daniele Covo.

Figure 2.2. Fredy Barouh in the British Royal Air Force Regiment, September 1944 to June 1945. Archive of Daniele Covo.

Fredy had an elder sister, Lily (Lou), born in November 1911. She got engaged to Henri Covo in Thessaloniki in February 1934 and married him in Athens in March 1934. The couple then moved to Paris and had their first daughter, Ginette Stella, who was born in October 1937. After the war began, the couple immigrated to Argentina in August 1941, first passing through Lyon (zone libre) then through Spain, where they took the boat in Barcelona with their daughter Ginette. A second daughter, Daniele, was born in Buenos Aires in December 1942. Ginette married Marcel Uziel in Athens in 1964, and the rest of the family returned back to Paris from Argentina in 1965. They have two sons. Henri Covo died in Paris in 1993, and Lily Covo née Barouh died in the same city in 2011, the year of her 100th birthday.

I had the honor of meeting Daniele Covo in Paris in 2019. She had come across the Greek edition of this book and expressed support for a publication in French and English. She also provided me with more letters that she had in her possession, as well as family photographs. Regrettably, Daniele passed away in Paris in 2020 and did not live to see this publication. Her nephew, Jacques Uziel, remains very supportive of this project, in her memory.

Figure 2.3. Mathilde Barouh and her children, Lily and Fredy. Archive of Daniele Covo.

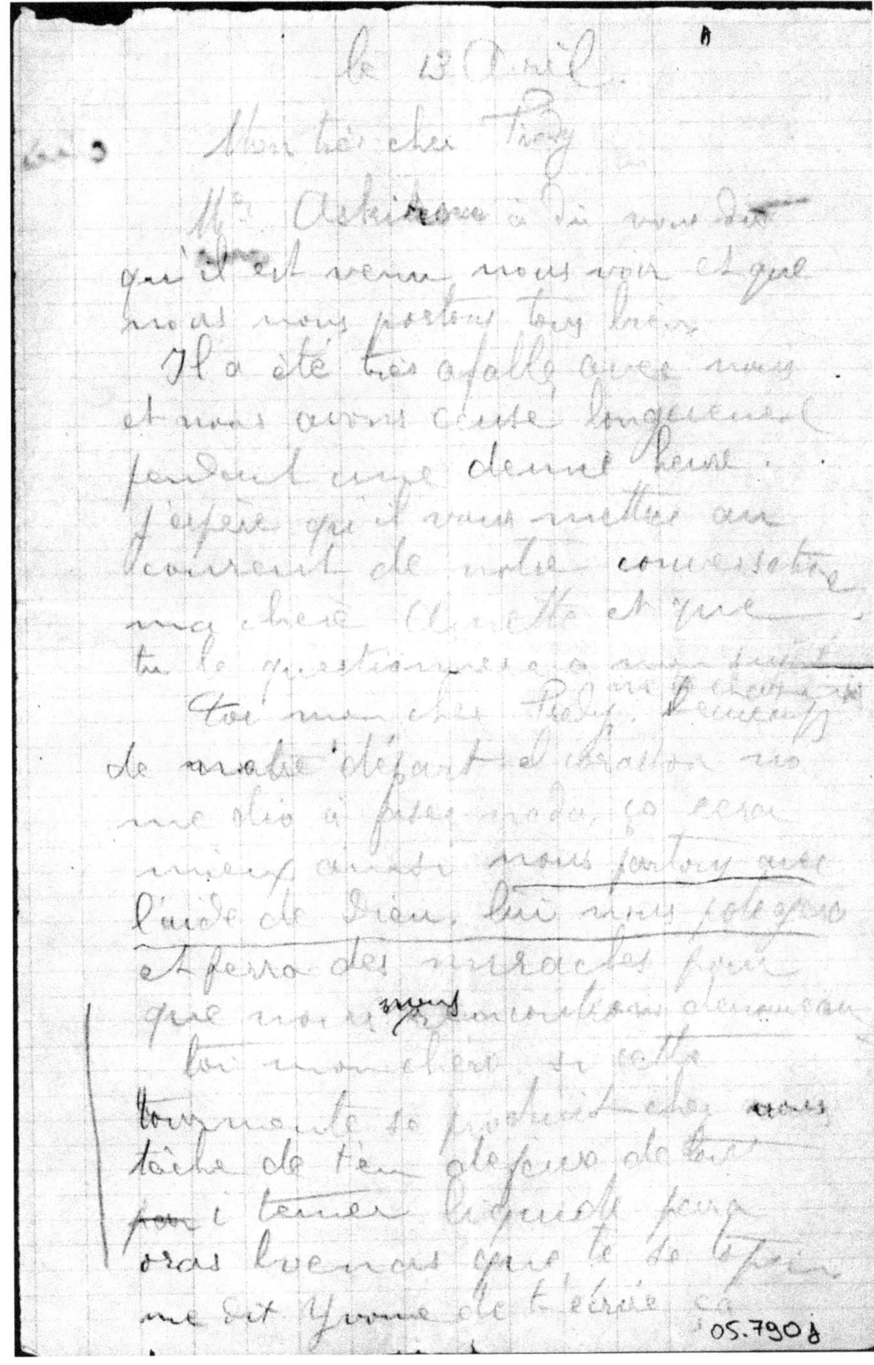

le 13 Avril.

Mon très cher Tredy

Mr Ashkenazi a dû vous dire qu'il est venu nous voir et que nous nous portons tous bien.

Il a été très affable avec nous et nous avons causé longuement pendant une demi heure.

J'espère qu'il vous mettra au courant de notre conversation

Figure 2.4. The first page of Mathilde Barouh's letter of 13 April 1943. Archive of the Jewish Museum of Greece.

Letters from Mathilde Barouh

Red Cross Telegram, from Matilde Barouh to Pitchon and Co, Buenos Aires, Argentina, 4 January 1943 (arrived in Geneva 12 February 1943)

Dear Henri, Lili,

We have received your letters, do not worry. Fredy still in Athens. We await news. Easy birth to Lily. Kiss Ginette, uncle,[1] family. Love from your mother.[2]

First Letter, Sunday, 28 February [1943]

(As you instructed, I haven't dated the letter from Lou. Add it yourself.)[3]

My dear Fredy,

I hope you received my letter of the 20th, and that you have an idea of what our life here is like.

With all that is happening,[4] I haven't been able to write to Lou yet for the birth.[5] At least you already did. I'm sure Mrs. Joseph wrote to them and that Lily, not having received a letter from me, will get all sorts of ideas. Enclosed, you will find a letter for her, which you must send without delay.

As you read in my letter, we live at Amalias Street No. 30, the address you must send your letters to from now on. We have a very large room, i.e. two rooms without a separating wall; we have four beds: two beds for Julenno, Yvonne, and Claude on one side, and two for aunt and me on the other side. The two opposite one another, a stove and a table in the middle for eating.

Right now, we're playing harakiri . . . Luckily, we live with people who are very nice. I think you know them: Gabriel Hassid,[6] a friend of Salamo's. For the time being, we are well. May something worse does not come to us.[7]

You understand that today it is harder than before with a life like this. Unfortunately, I had already told you before you left the last time that things could come and we would find one here and the other there.[8]

You told me you're planning on getting a permit.[9] It's physically impossible to get one at the moment. What God says, this will happen.[10] Just make sure you don't leave me without a letter.

You wrote in your last letter that you received my letter as well as one for Mrs. Estrea. I wrote to Mrs. Estrea twice. What happened to my first letter? I fear that not all my letters, which Salamo sends by post through Pepo or Alberto, are sent because you often tell me you don't receive news from me.

Try to keep up with what's going on here. Did you receive the letter in which I tell you to write to Sami and thank him for thinking of me? Let me know. I have so much to tell you, but I can't do it by letter. Just wait, ichalla,[11] and one day we will be reunited. We have so many things to talk about.

Kiss dear Annette, Henri, and Djiko. I send you all my love, my darling Fredy.

[attached letter, sent later to Argentina]

My dearest Henry and Lily,

Besides hearing the good news of the birth, my dear Lily, we haven't received any other news from you. I hope that you're all ok. Thank God we're doing well over here.

I wrote several letters to you, my darlings. I don't know if you received them. Don't worry about us, my darlings, we are all well, and so is Fredy in Athens.

How are the dear children? Ginette is a big girl now and must be happy to have a little sister.

Kiss them for me.

Kisses to both of you,
Your mother

Second Letter, 15 March [1943]

My darling Fredy,

We haven't received any news from you for more than three weeks, and with what's happening to us here, I'm terribly worried.

You know what's going on, no doubt, and all the more reason for you to write to me every two days, if possible, so that I can read your letters before our unfortunate departure.

Who would have thought I would be so cruelly separated from you, my darling, and without much hope of ever seeing you again? How will aunt and I be able to bear what awaits us at our age?

I could have been with you for a long time, and now I'm leaving. Only God knows for how long.

I went to see Gedaliah in person yesterday for the two pieces of tissue, because she still hasn't given them to me. Ino brought them over this morning.

I don't know what I'm writing about to you. My hand is trembling and my eyes are blurry.

My dear Annette, you must take care of Fredy the way you always have. Try to keep him from getting too sad; let us have hope in God that one day we will meet again.

I leave you, my darlings, and kiss all four of you with an aching heart.

Your aunt and mother

Third Letter, 18 March [1943]

My dearest Fredy,

Sarina just received a letter from Denyse in which she writes that you are very worried about not receiving any news from me. I wrote several letters to you. Why didn't you receive them?

We haven't heard from you for the past fifteen days. Write to us at 32 Amalias Street[12] or at Sarina's.

I wrote to Lou today because I don't know if I'll be able to write to her later. Try to write to me every two days, so that I receive your letter before I leave.

My dear Annette, you must take care of my darling Fredy the way you always have. You have been so good to us. You and Henri must not let him panic.

We are all well. Tender kisses to the four of you from your aunt and mother.

Fourth Letter, 23 March [1943]

My dearest Fredy,

I received both of your letters dated the 15th and the 19th, and they reassured me because I hadn't received any news from you for more than twenty days.

Mrs. Hajinikolaou told us to call immediately, and Tida Saporta[13] came on Sunday morning to tell us that you had called and that there was hope. May it please God that this comes true.

I can't even begin to tell you, my darling Fredy, how frightened we all are, especially me who could have—and should have—been with you a long time ago.

You should write to Salamo to give him courage and because I am under their wing. You must do so right away.

I wrote you several letters. You haven't told me whether you received them or not.

My dear Annette, I wonder how you all are as everyone has dear ones leaving over here. How will poor father, who is so old and despondent, be able to bear this ordeal?

I went to Dr. Alevi[14] today to get the telephone number. You can only call us[15] once from his place so that I can hear your voice, my darling Fredy: 80-121. You can call in the morning between 9 and 10.

Try to write to me very often, my darling. Embrace dear Henri, Annette, and Djico. Kisses from me.

Your mother

Mrs. Eftihia has allowed us to use her phone only once. You can call more often at Sam Saporta's.

Fifth Letter, 1 April [1943]

My dearest Fredy,

This morning, I received your letter of the 26th in which you say you wrote two letters to Salamo. Fortunately, the third one arrived. It was about time.

You don't mention Mr. Scaravolo. Has he renounced the project? It would be better for him to put it off until later.

You tell me to be courageous and patient. I can't be either, anymore. Not knowing what will happen is agony for us. May God give us patience to be able to tolerate what awaits us and not to die far from you my darling Fredy.[16]

Sometimes I have hope things will be like before—that we will be near one another, with me enjoying your presence, loving you as before. I am so unlucky being far away from you when we could have been close to each other with everything we spend.

This separation has ruined us. Nothing has been left to us anymore. Everything has frayed like cloth. There is nothing else left other than what I will take with me. The houses have been emptied with the horror that from one moment to the next we could leave.

I already wrote to you that they took Beni and Arie. You can imagine how unfortunate are Louisa and the aunt. All the time crying, which breaks your heart when you see them. I hope God will guard them and keep them safe, amen.[17]

We wait for you to call us every day. You say it's difficult to call in the morning. Call us any time up until 5 o'clock, because we can't go out after 5 o'clock any longer.

I haven't heard any more news from dear Henry, dear Lily . . . She'd die if she knew how far away you are from me during these moments. She would never forgive you for having left me alone, depressed and living with others for so long.

What is done is done. When the person has no luck, he is thrown to the sea.[18] This is my case. All the same, I'll try to hold up for longer in the hope of seeing you again, my darlings.

I often see Salamo, dearest Annette. He comes by almost every day. He said he spoke to you on the phone. He, too, like everyone: nothing has been left to him.[19]

I also see Jacques. He passes by here every day. He's doing well.

Kisses to dear Henri, Djiko, and both of you.

All my love,
Your aunt and mother

Sixth Letter, Sunday, 4 April [1943]

My dearest Fredy,

I received your letter of 31 March in which you tell me that you're doing all you can to help us. Unfortunately, we have lost all hope because yesterday they blocked the Aroestu[20] side and took everyone they found there. Salamo, Rebecca, the children, and uncle are already at Baron Hirsch.[21] It will be our turn any moment.

Today, Mrs. Eftihia allowed us to use the phone. We waited for a long time, and so Yvonne asked the switchboard, and they told us the line was busy, so you can imagine the state we were in when we left.

Even though I know I wouldn't have been able to talk to you, I would have heard your beloved voice—the voice I have missed for so long. We hope you'll give us another call tomorrow.

I was about to send you a small photo when your letter arrived, in which you ask me for one. I couldn't get a new one taken right away because there's no photographer around here. I'm sending you the photo of a young mother, the one who still had all the courage and patience to raise you as I did. Now, I no longer have the courage or the patience to endure this ordeal. May God help me endure in order to see you all again, my darlings.

I saw Pepo today. He passes by our house every day. His address is Parodos Miaoulis 3. Write to him without fail.

This might be the last letter I write to you, my darling. Remind me, Anette or you by phone, the good memories from all of our loved ones. I always have fond memories of the Covos. They have always shown me affection.

Did you receive any other news from our loved ones? I wish I could read them one more time.

My dear Annette, I entrust Fredy to you. You and Henry know how to keep him from getting too upset. Ichalla that God will make it easier and we will meet again soon, amen.

In the name of God we will go, he who gives force and health and will soon bring calm to the world to see your faces one more time. To call Victorine and the Covos on the phone to tell them so long, ichalla.[22]
Kisses to Henry, Djiko, and both of you.

With all my love,
Your aunt and mother

[note on the first page] Give my love to Raphael, Marie, Frida Saporta, Uncle Gabriel . . .

Seventh Letter, Wednesday, 7 April [1943]

My dearest Annette, Henri, Fredy, and Djiko,

It seems that we're leaving the day after tomorrow. I send you my love to all of you one last time, to you my darling whom I have loved so. Being separated from you is killing me. I'll try to withstand this ordeal in the hope that we'll be reunited one day, my darling Fredy. I'll wait for your letter today so as to hear from you and feel you close to me once again. I imagine how anxious you must be feeling without me by your side, but that's how it is.

We're busy preparing food today. We don't know what else to do, how to carry all this on the back. There are some moments that we start to cry with the misfortune that has got to us.[23]

Before finishing this letter, the postman brought me your dear letter. I had lost all hope since it was already past midday.

I read your letter, Fredy darling, and I bitterly regret having caused you sorrow. I was so nervous and desperate the day I struck out at you. I know you were a very affectionate son to your mother, my darling, but things are such that I am far from you. As you say my darling, let us have faith in God that one blessed day we will be together again, and that love and tenderness will make us forget everything.

Dear Annette, I have no doubt that you'll continue to love Fredy as you've always loved him. I leave you all, my darlings, and send you all my love.

To you, my darling Fredy, I send my blessings, with my affection and tenderness. May you be happy, and may God protect you all until the end, amen.

Your mother

Eighth Letter, Saturday, 10 April [1943]

My dearest Annette,

The brother-in-law of this gentleman gave me your letter, one for Jacques as well, and I immediately gave them both to Mathilde.

Jacques came to see me in the afternoon, to give him the address of this gentleman. We left together but we didn't find him at his house. His brother-in-law told me that he would arrive last night after 7:00 or this morning, but he hasn't. This morning, Jacques came by to inquire as to whether I had seen him. I told him no, and he went to his place. I don't know if he saw him.

Regarding what you wrote to me about, my dear Annette, Fredy knows it's impossible for me at the moment. I'll wait until he comes, otherwise I'll go to his place again to find him.

The postman just brought me your letter, my dear Fredy, as well Salamo's, dated the 7th.

Your loving letter of today made me shed many tears. There are times when I feel I'm failing, my darling, and there are moments of hope when I believe I'll see you again and be with you. You're my only reason for living. I often think of how this news will alarm our dear Lily and Henry.

If I don't come back, my darling Fredy, do everything you can—should you have the means later on—to go see them and, if possible, to live close to them or near our dear Annette and Henry, who are like brothers to you. They love you, and you'll have some affection close to you. Just be brave of all the misfortune that will befall us.

We might still be here for another two or three days. Contact Mrs. Gentille to see whether we have left, so that you no longer have to write to me.

Yesterday I saw Pepo Plerinti. He gave me candy from the wedding of Sarica and Mr. Assael, the leather merchant. They got married on Wednesday, and tomorrow Pepo is getting married to Miss Haim, Ellio Haim's youngest sister.[24] They spend every day together here. It appears that married couples have certain advantages compared to young, single people.

We hope you'll be spared until the end over there. In case the same thing happens to you my dearest Annette, you must find him a companion—a young girl worthy of him—with my blessing.

It's already been eight days since Salamo and his family left. They should have already arrived. May it please God that they had a tolerable trip.

I can't write anymore, my darlings. I'm leaving and embrace you all with the same affection I have for Fredy.

Your aunt and mother

Ninth Letter, 13 April [1943]

My dearest Fredy,

Mr. Askirou must have told you he came to see us, and that we are all well. He was very amiable toward us, and we spoke at length for half an hour. I hope he'll fill you in on our conversation, my dear Annette, and that you'll ask him about me.

Don't grieve too much upon our departure, my dear Fredy. I didn't have the heart to do anything.[25] It's better this way. We're leaving with God's help. He'll protect us and perform miracles so that we meet each other again.

If this misfortune should reach you, my dear, make sure you unravel yourself from everything and have cash in case you need it.[26] Yvonne told me to tell you this.

Perhaps this is the last letter I'll write to you, my darling Annette. Fredy must not grieve. Let's hope that God will reunite us again.

I leave you, my dearest Annette, Henri, Fredy, and Djiko, and I embrace all four of you with the same affection.

Your aunt and mother

My blessing and one last kiss to my darling Fredy.

[the same letter continues on a different sheet of paper]

Before giving the letter to Benico, I received your letter of the 9th in which you tell me that two of your acquaintances will come by with news of you. He'll also go see Mr. Benveniste.

If I knew where I could find Mr. Benveniste today, I'd go see him, but at the moment we don't know who has left, who's still here. If I knew where I could find him, I'd go see him right away to find out if this gentleman has been to his place. No one has come to see us yet.

I saw Pepo Plerinti. He told me he received your letter. You probably know that Sarica has gotten married to a Mr. Assael, leather merchant, and that Pepo is getting married to Elio Haim's youngest sister. They gave me wedding favors. They were supposed to get married on Sunday, but the wedding was postponed and will be held one of these days.

And to yours, my soul, with calmness in the world and all together.[27]

We believe we'll be leaving today. We'll be leaving very soon. Maybe tomorrow. We don't know anything.

Remind me of the good memories of our loved ones, including Rebeca and Simon, to whom we owe the happiness of our dearest Lou. Try to write to our darlings from time to time.

I'm sending you a million kisses,
Your mother

[Continued in a different handwriting]

My dearest Fredy,

As mother is writing to you, I decided to write a few lines, too. We're in perfect health, and fortunately our morale is high, despite all the misfortunes that have befallen us. You probably received a letter from Solomon. He's also very brave, and I hope that one day the Good Lord will help us see each other again, and that he will protect us until the very end.

Best wishes to everyone at home.
I embrace you fondly.

Tenth Letter, [mid-April 1943]

My dearest Annette,

Mr. Askirou came to see me. He was very nice to me, but there's nothing he can do, unfortunately.

Regarding the other gentleman Fredy writes about, I saw him as well, but he was cold to me.[28]

We're leaving with the help of God, and in the hope of seeing you again.

Kisses from your aunt to all of you.

Eleventh Letter, 17 April [1943]

My dear Fredy,

I'm taking advantage of Mr. Blejen being here, to write a few lines to you.

I hope you received all my letters. I believe you saw Mr. Askirou, and that he relayed our conversation to you.

We're still here. Mr. Blejen will inform you of our departure.

Goodbye, my darling Fredy. We'll meet each other later with the help of God.

I embrace you with all my heart,
Your mother

Letter from Fredy Barouh and Albertos, 25 May/7 June 1943

25 May 1943[29]
My dearest Henry and Lily,

I just received this letter from mother, which I now hasten to send to you. You can imagine our joy upon receiving a letter from dear Henri dated 15 March, ten days ago. None of your letters mention my letters or mother's. However, God knows how often we wrote to you. I hope this one will reach you at least.

Ginette must be a big girl by now. We're dying to see a picture of Danielle. Who does she look like? Is she blonde or brunette? Mother asked me in her last letter.

Here, we are in good health, thank God. Everyone is fine at Annette's—they send you kisses.

Be sure to write to us as often as you can, and above all, tell us whether you received my letters.

Embrace my dear nieces for me. Lots of love from your Fredy.

7 June 1943
My warmest regards and best wishes to all. Write to us as often as you can.
Albertos[30]

Notes

1. Could refer to Salomon Covo, a brother of Henri Covo's father, who had just arrived at Buenos Aires with his wife and two daughters.
2. Written on a Red Cross standard form (form 61) which allows for 25-word civilian messages with "family news of strictly personal character." Archive of Daniele Covo.
3. Letter follows. Sent from Fredy Barouh to his sister Lily Covo in Argentina, June 1943. Archive of Daniele Covo.
4. She refers to the transfer to the ghetto and the implementation of the anti-Jewish measures. Sentence in Judeo-Spanish.
5. Daniele Covo was born in Argentina in December 1943.
6. Gabriel Hassid, of Haim and Gioia, was born in 1900. His wife was named Ester Angel and his son was named Haim, born in 1939. All were victims of the Holocaust.
7. Sentence in Judeo-Spanish.
8. Paragraph in Judeo-Spanish.
9. To be able to travel to Athens.
10. Sentence in Judeo-Spanish.
11. *Inshallah*, "God willing" in Arabic.
12. Written in Greek script.
13. The wife of Sam Saporta, mentioned at the bottom of the letter. They were deported to the Bergen-Belsen camp, being Spanish citizens, and survived the war.
14. Raphael Alevi, of Yeshoula and Mazaltov, and his wife Eftihia née Matsa. Their son survived.
15. Greek expression translated in French.
16. Sentence in Judeo-Spanish.
17. Two paragraphs in Judeo-Spanish.
18. Sentence in Judeo-Spanish.
19. Sentence in Judeo-Spanish.
20. Location inside a Jewish neighborhood.
21. Transit camp opposite of the train station.
22. Two paragraphs written in Judeo-Spanish.
23. Sentences in Judeo-Spanish.
24. Ellio (Elias) Haim, born in 1911, had to sisters and a brother. The youngest, Sylvia, was born in 1923. Pepo Parente was born in 1911. Only Ellio survived the camps, returned to Thessaloniki and migrated to the US.
25. Sentence in Judeo-Spanish.
26. Sentence in Judeo-Spanish.
27. Sentence in Judeo-Spanish.
28. Expression in Judeo-Spanish.

29. This letter was written on the other side of Mathilde Barouh's letter of 28 February 1943, that was sent to her daughter in Argentina.
30. Unknown.

Part III

Cazes Letters

Introduction

Leon Saltiel

A first collection of six letters by Neama Cazes written in Thessaloniki during the German occupation were given to the archive of the Jewish Museum of Greece in 1992. Its director at the time, Nikos Stavroulakis, published an English translation of the letters in the museum's newsletter. In his introduction, we learn that

> In 1942, [Neama] had gone to Athens to rent a room for herself and one of her sons, in the home of a Christian, Mrs. Eleni Chatzimihail. The other son had remained in Salonika. Late in 1942, Neama then returned to Salonika to pack up her things and return to Athens with her other son. It appears she was caught in Salonika in the initial round-up of Jews in three ghettos established to facilitate their deportation. Her son managed to escape and make his way to Athens to join his brother. [. . .] Nothing is known of the fate of Neama, nor that of her two sons, Maurice and Berto. The letters were discovered only two years ago [in 1990], when Mrs. Chatzimihail emptied her house prior to its demolition to make way for an apartment building. On realizing what they were, she gave them to some Jewish friends who in turn passed them on to the museum.[1]

Initially, we knew very little about this woman, not even her last name. Nevertheless, with the help of Aliki Arouh, the archivist of the Jewish Community of Thessaloniki, we were able to identify her. Neama Cazes was born in 1889 and was the daughter of Avraam and Mazaltov Djivre. Her husband, Yehuda (Juda) Cazes, had died in 1935. He had seven siblings: Samuel (who died before the war), Albert (who died in

Figure 3.1. Neama Cazes. Archive of Matilda Chrysochoou.

1917), Palomba, Mathilde, Menahem, Haïm, and Binouta. The family had its origins in the city of Komotini, in the northeast part of Greece. Neama's two sons were born there, Maurice in 1911 and Alberto in 1916. After a few years, they moved to Thessaloniki.

In 2003, Ms. Chatzimihail made a second donation to the Jewish Museum of Greece, and only recently was it linked to the first donation, thus coming to our knowledge thanks to the digitization of the archive. Ms. Eleni-Ioanna Chatzimihail, née Epitropou, was the sister of Fani Epitropou, the wife of Maurice Cazes. In memory of her sister, Ms. Chatzimihail made this second donation, which included letters between members of the Cazes family dating as early as 1924, education certificates, and information on Maurice Cazes and his activities during the Greco-Italian War, the German occupation, and the resistance. This new material allows us to correct and complete the introduction by Stavroulakis.

Maurice Cazes studied at the French high school of Thessaloniki, Lycée Français. From his grades from 1923–24, we learn that he was a very good student and had received an honor for his performance. On 6 October 1932, Cazes joined the army, serving the biggest part of the time at the Eleventh General Staff Office of the Third Army Corps in Thessaloniki. After his release on 6 December 1933, he worked initially in insurance and, from 1935, in the Romanian oil company Steaua.

Around 1936–37, he met his future wife, Fani Epitropou. The Epitropou family had come to Thessaloniki in 1929 from the region of Eastern Rumelia in modern-day Bulgaria and settled in the district of Vasilissis Olgas-Analipsi. Fani, known as Fanoula, graduated from the Schinas School and studied tailoring in Thessaloniki, while in 1935–36 she studied haute couture in the Tsopanelli fashion house in Athens. In 1939, Maurice Cazes, Fani, and her family settled in Athens.

On 25 August 1940, Maurice Cazes was mobilized as a reserve corporal in the 3rd Company of the 50th Infantry Regiment, two months before the declaration of the Greco-Italian War on 28 October 1940. During the military operations, he participated in many battles, where he was distinguished "for his bravery, courage and initiative," having many successes. Indeed, in October 1990, in an article in *Sunday Vima* with the title "How I Did Not Take Over Korytsa [Korçë]," he described the reconnaissance operation he conducted with a small team before the entrance of the Greek army into the city on 22 November 1940.

On 26 April 1941, he was dismissed from the army and returned to Athens, where his mother was already located. Initially, they stayed at the home of the Epitropou family in Kallithea and then in other neigh-

Figure 3.2. Neama and Juda Cazes. Archive of Marie Cazes.

boring homes. On 18 September 1941, Neama Cazes left for Thessaloniki for a few days, with the goal to bring food for her family in Athens. However, due to the difficulties of transportation and because she did not have a special permit, she could not return to Athens and was blocked in Thessaloniki. She initially stayed there with her second son Berto (Alberto), and together they wrote the first letters to Maurice in Athens. Berto left for Athens toward the end of February 1943, after the imposition of the first anti-Jewish measures. Notwithstanding Maurice's efforts, Neama could not return to Athens. She was arrested by the Nazis and transferred to Auschwitz, where she perished.

In Athens, Maurice Cazes continued to work for Steaua. After the Italian capitulation and the entrance of the Germans into Athens, Maurice worked for a short time in the harbor of Piraeus with fake papers; on 6 October 1943, he went to the mountains of Pelion to serve as an interpreter and link of the guerrilla forces of EAM-ELAS[2] with the General Headquarters of the Middle East Forces of the Allies, i.e. the British. He participated in military operations against the Germans—including acts of sabotage and bombings of train lines and bridges—and in efforts to supply goods to ELAS and Allied ships. In August 1944, Fani joined him in the mountains where the couple would be unofficially married. From 9 October 1944, Maurice worked as an interpreter for the British Army until 5 December, when he resigned. On the eve of Dekemvriana, the December 1944 clashes in Athens, he returned to that city.

After the liberation of the country, Maurice and Fani got married in Athens, and Maurice got baptized in the Greek Orthodox tradition under the name "Antonios." In 1945, he assumed high responsibilities in the newly founded BP oil company, where he worked until 1975, serving as its Greek director. Throughout these years, Maurice distinguished himself for his integrity, perceptiveness, and sense of justice in dealing with matters related to managing the company. Because of his position and responsibilities, the couple made many trips both inside and outside of Greece. From her side, Fani organized the social events for the company, especially for the children and the staff of BP.

Maurice spoke many languages: Greek, French, English, Hebrew, Turkish, Italian, and Esperanto. He was an admirer of ancient Greece, of Greek nature and Greek culture. Through BP, he organized the first rally racing events in Greece, where he also participated as a consultant—and as a participant. He was one of the main founding members of the camping "Meltemi," designed for the oil company employees and located in Rafina, Attica. As a member of the Greek Mountaineering Club, the Greek Tour Club, and the Automobile and Touring Club of Greece (ELPA), as well as privately, he traveled across Greece and pho-

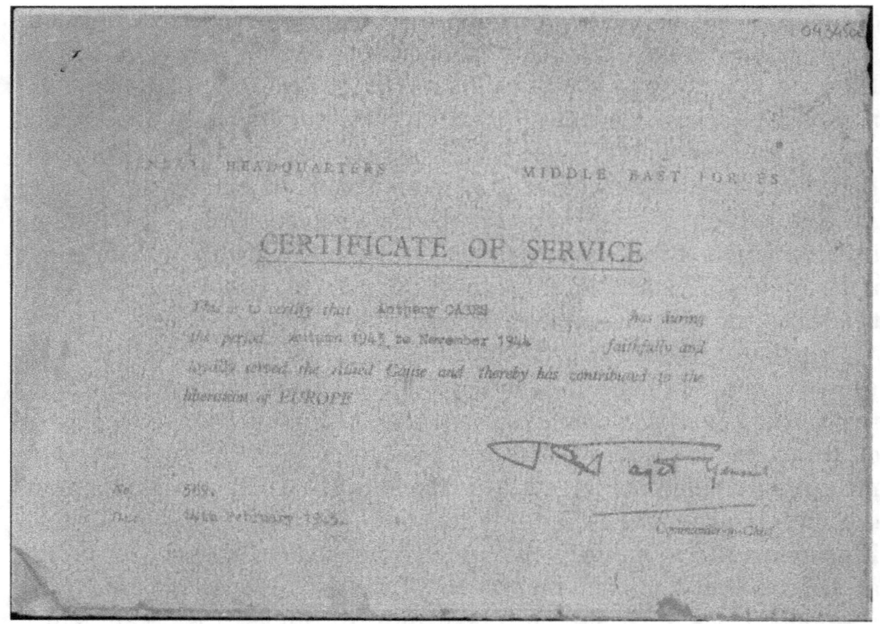

[illegible] HEADQUARTERS MIDDLE EAST FORCES

CERTIFICATE OF SERVICE

This is to certify that Anthony CAZES *has during the period* Autumn 1943 to November 1944 *faithfully and loyally served the Allied Cause and thereby has contributed to the liberation of* EUROPE

No. 589.

Date 14th February 1945.

Commander-in-Chief

Figure 3.3. Certificate of Service of the General Headquarters of the Middle East Forces, to Maurice (Anthony) Cazes for his contribution "to the liberation of Europe," 14 February 1945. Archive of the Jewish Museum of Greece.

tographed an extensive variety of the Greek fauna. He collected wildflowers from all areas of the country, and he donated this archive to the University of Thessaloniki. For his resistance actions, Maurice Cazes was honored by both the British Army and the Prefecture of Magnisia in a special ceremony in August 1986. He died in Paris in 1991 due to a postoperative complication. His body was transferred to Athens where he was buried. Fani Cazes died in 2002.

His brother, Albertos Cazes, survived the German occupation in Athens using false papers under the name Nikolaos Chatzimihail. The Chatzimihail family had very cordial relations with the Epitropou family, as they both originated from the same area, Stenimachos of East Romelia, and resided in the same area, Kallithea in Athens. Nikolaos Chatzimihail was a cousin of the family who had been killed in Drama during the Bulgarian atrocities of September 1941. Albertos took over his identity and kept the name Nikos even after the war. He ran a furniture shop in Kallithea and was very skilled in wood carving. He was very well educated and circulated among intellectual circles, with whose members he had close relations, among them the Greek poet Odysseus Elytis who was awarded the Nobel Prize in Literature in 1979. He got

Figure 3.4. Top row, from left to right: Nektarios and Matilda Chrysochoou, Albertos and Ioanna Cazes, Matilda's parents. Second row: Fani Cazes, Jo Nahmias and his daughter, Renee, from Paris, and Maurice Cazes. Photograph from the wedding of Matilda Cazes with Nektarios Chrysochoou, 1975. Archive of Matilda Chrysochoou.

married in 1947 and was baptized in the Greek Orthodox tradition. He died in 1988. Today his daughter and grandchildren live in Athens.

The letters that follow were kindly provided by the Jewish Museum of Greece and come from the two donations made by Eleni Chatzimihail. In addition, this English edition of the book includes letters provided by the Cazes family in Paris that did not appear in the original Greek edition.

Note

1. Stavroulakis, "Letters," 5–6.
2. The National Liberation Front (EAM) was the largest resistance organization in Greece and was primarily affiliated with the Communist Party of Greece (KKE). The Greek People's Liberation Army (ELAS) was EAM's military wing, which became the largest armed guerrilla force in the country fighting against the Axis occupation.

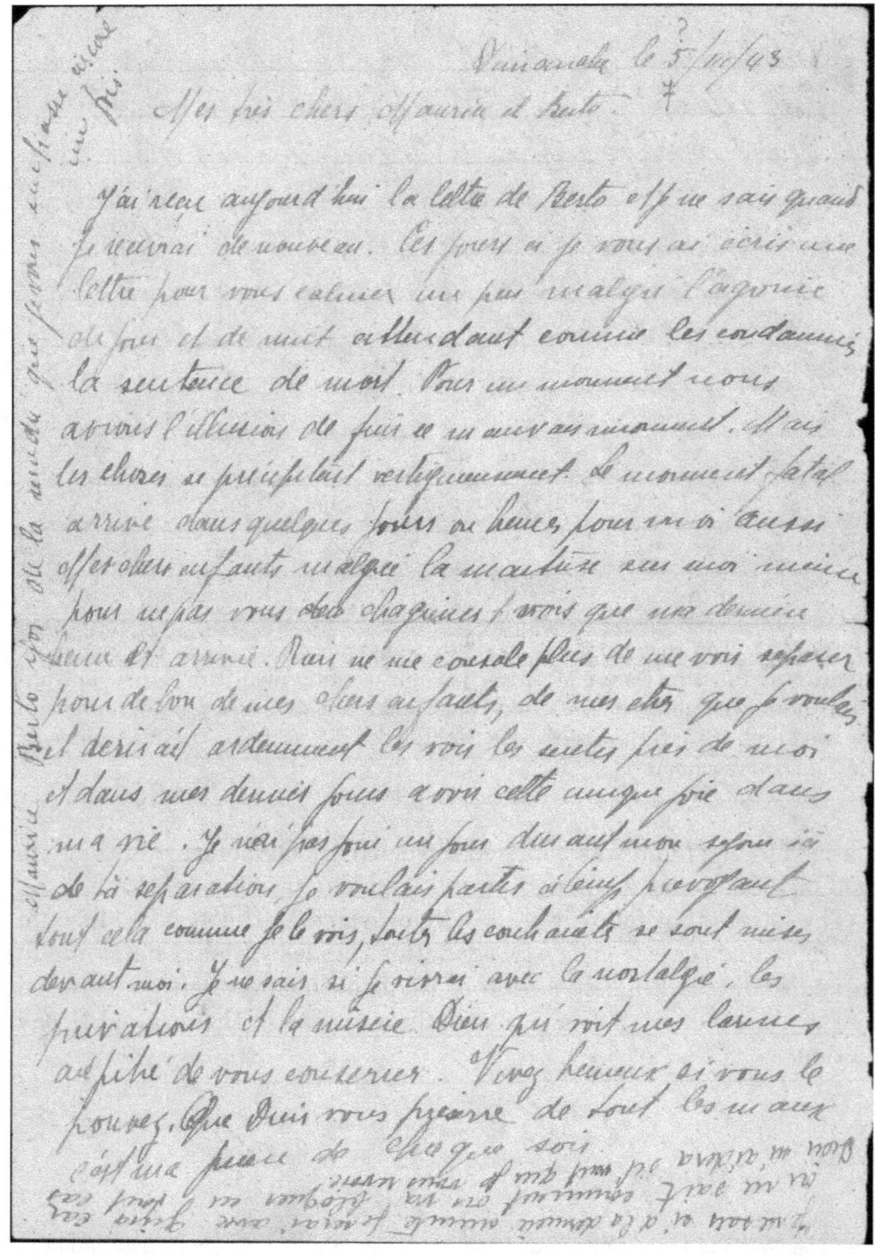

Figure 3.5. The first page of Neama Cazes's letter of 5 March 1943. Archive of the Jewish Museum of Greece.

LETTERS FROM NEAMA CAZES

First Letter, Friday, 29 January 1943

To read the letter, place it on a piece of paper[1]

My dearest Maurice,

You should have received my letter by now. I don't remember the date, and yesterday I received your card in which you tell me that you're doing well. I'm waiting to receive the long letter you promised me either tomorrow or on Sunday.

Soon, I'll have finished ironing and cleaning the kitchen. Berto hasn't come to eat yet, and it's 2:30 p.m. It's payday. I'm taking the opportunity to write to you so that I can tell you what I'm doing. Ever since it snowed five days ago, everything has turned to ice, and the roads are like mirrors. It's freezing cold, and it's very windy, too. The owner lights the stove every Friday evening, and we shiver like a bunch of wet cats. Luckily, the brazier helps a bit as it heats us in front and from behind. We try to keep as warm as possible in bed.

You asked me what kind of blanket we have: Berto covers himself with the woolen blanket, and I cover myself with a baby blanket, the carpet from the chest, my sport coat and Berto's raincoat. The thought of having to get up in the morning and moving from one place to another in the cold gives me the goosebumps. I'm sitting next to the brazier at the moment and writing to you. The snow has covered half of the wall of the room where we sleep, and we breathe very well. I went to get Saturday's provisions this morning, because we risk getting excommunicated for cooking on that day.[2]

They requisitioned the small room where we eat. I wasn't at home at the time, and Daisy was so scared she let them have their way without putting up a fight. We don't know who will come and cook there on Saturday. Maybe he'll eat garlic and cross himself.[3] Yousse and his wife nearly went crazy last night.

They made me so angry that I went out despite the cold. When I got home, I saw them kneeling with their heads bowed in desperation and sadness. They looked like Karaginos and Hadjivat,[4] with Berto doing the miming. I nearly ripped my lip trying to keep myself from laughing. We'll see now how many people they'll bring. Our house is at the Gouzios Cleantos Italias crossroads.[5]

Gina isn't working at the workshop because it has been leased to a butcher.

Regarding our health—we're well and we've started to buy oil; today I made a pastelico of potatoes[6] with oil (heavy for machines) from the grocer's.

Let me know what the result is for my permit.[7] What are you eating? Did you look for the shoes? What condition are the shirts in?

Last night, I dreamt of you, and you were in a good mood, making roskitas.[8] My son,[9] when will we be able to make good things together again?

Today, I felt a little more hopeful, but it didn't last long. Berto gave me 3,000 drachmas to buy a pair of stockings for the house. I try to keep the one I have in good condition for going out. Isn't Cantas coming? Send my best regards to him and his landlords, too.

I embrace you with all my heart. Your mother who adores you and hopes to see you one day.

Neama

Letter from Berto, Saturday, 30 January 1943

My dearest Maurice,

Today, Saturday, Gina will pick me up from the office so that we can buy a pair of stockings for mother. Tomorrow, Sunday, we'll be waiting for news from you, as usual.

We received your card the day before yesterday, and we're writing to you before receiving your news so that we don't delay writing to you.

Business is very calm this week. It's very difficult to sell shoe polish. (Sale: two dozen, approximately 1,800 in consignment stock.)

Ditto for soap:[10] The market is full of soap vendors. Only very small amounts are being sold. Tomorrow, I'll go to the village with Mario to sell soap. Here is the good soap![11]

In comparison, provisions are affordable. Detailed prices: Bread 1,200. Oil 6,000–6,200. Potatoes 750–900. Beans 1,600–1,800. Sugar 16,000. Cheese 10,000. Carob[12] 3,800 etc. etc. Soap 4,500! Tell me what your prices are, too. Halva 8,000. Meat 6–8,000. Fish from 2,500 (sazan). We sometimes eat meat. We forgot what it tasted like the past eight months.

Concerning the debts: Mario 15,000—Gina 4. That's all.

I hope I'll be able to get by this week with the weekly salary,[13] and possibly, your check.[14] With your checks and my salary, I might balance my budget. I'll pay off Moris' debt etc., with the profit I make from the soap.

Everything is fine, Madame la Marquise.[15]

Did you buy the shoes? My laced boots look like old shoes.

Cantas: The invisible man.

Gina sends you her regards.

I hug you dearly,
Berthy

N.B. Don't get upset over the letter paper mother used. This is the last of it.[16]
So long.[17]

Second Letter, Wednesday, 3 February 1943

My beloved Maurice,

You've probably received the three letters of ours in which I tell you we're doing very well. We're worried you're receiving our letters late.

I wrote to you when it snowed, last Friday. Fortunately, the weather has changed but it's still a bit foggy. We can go out on the street and get some sun, if there's any. They told me it snowed at your place, too.

Yesterday, a man came by—instead of Cantas, whom we had waited for in vain—and brought me the calcium shots Mr. Dingas had requested. Thank you very much, my dear Maurice, I'll try to take them as soon as I can.

On Sunday, I was with Dora at the Saporta home. Mr. Yeni sends you his greetings.

On Sunday, we also had Gina stay and dine with us. The menu was slightly more elaborate than usual. A little sazan with plums, the pastelico of potatoes that I wrote to you about on Friday, and a salad. For the first time since the beginning of the war, we had a dozen of ferik apples (at 1,500/oke)[18] in your honor for dessert. Imagine, my dear Maurice, how much I was thinking of you, and of your love of pastelico even though it didn't turn out that great. What are you eating?

Are you getting things with coupons?[19] The law hasn't been enforced here yet. Let us pray to God that the war will end soon and that we will get over it.[20]

Did you buy the shoes? Try to buy them as soon as possible.

The prices of items here are dropping at an alarming rate, especially food items. They're dropping by one thousand drachmas per day, not by one hundred per day. According to Berto, we cannot circulate in the market, but I haven't been able to go see for myself.

The tram ticket costs 150 drachmas. I was thinking of going to see Mrs. Avayou; apart from the 200 drachmas[21] for the tram, we arrive at home with an unraveled sleeve and missing buttons.

It was sunny yesterday, so we went for a ride to Salamine[22] with Mrs. Schaky, and then we went to her place.

I saw Algava who asked me to give you his greetings.

Alice seems calmer now that she had her bad teeth taken out.

We were told that Heuriette will return with her brother one of these days. Her mother is still in bed with jaundice, and in a pitiful state. I visit her once a week at 11 o'clock and quickly return home because the trams are crowded.

Tina sends you her warmest regards.

I'm writing to you in great detail because I don't have a lot to do. I'm waiting for Berto who hasn't arrived yet. It's 1:30. I've finished my work, and I'm relaxing a little.

I've been waiting a long time for the long letter you promised me. When I receive a letter from you, it feels like you're with me for one or two days. Then your vision begins to fade, and it feels as if I'm very far away from you my son.[23] Your pajama bottoms are still hanging, and it's as if you were here.

I'll leave the second sheet of paper for Berto—he wants to write to you about his work. Be well my dear Maurice, and may God quickly reunite all three of us in a happy home. I love and kiss you with all my heart.

Your mother,
Neama

The tenants of the requisitioned room haven't yet arrived.

Mrs. Lucie Angel,[24] whom I wrote to you about, left already fifteen days ago. You can get news from us through her. Her husband's, Isaac Angel, office is at 4 Miltiadi Street.

Letter from Berto continuing on the same paper, Thursday, 4 February 194[3]

My dearest Maurice,

I'm very worried and curious about whether you received my last letters, especially the long one I wrote one month ago on several green-colored sheets of paper, and which took me a whole morning to finish.

As mother informed you, we're very well. I'm still waiting for your answer to the question I asked you, and which I explained to you in detail, regarding Vito and Mario's situation.

Tram: 150 drachmas!! I go on foot every day.

Weather: Always superb.

Vito: I'm thinking of paying off his debt as soon as possible so that I won't have to pay later the owed money[25] and to remain true to my word.[26] I want to show him that I'm not like the others he lent money to and lost. Today, that money has increased in value, and Vito is no longer short of money (so to say).[27] This is a great opportunity.

Polish: Nobody buys it in large quantities today. I put the goods in consignment at Elie Suegor's and in Michel's store. The market is calm.

Soap: We have a little shop at "Capan" (Aristotelous),[28] and we'll sell it in okes. There's a lot of soap and other good stuff at the market. This is the first week we have a stall there, and I get home around 3:30–4:00 p.m. The result is quite satisfactory at the moment.

Mother: being separated from you is very difficult for her. Try to write to her a little more often. She's become very sensitive, and this bothers me a lot especially as I suffer from anxiety myself (as I told you). Anyway, let's move on . . .

I haven't seen Angela's husband, nor do I want to see him.

Esther: Do you think her marriage will end well?

Did Mousitza pay you?

Gina is doing well and sends you her greetings.

I'm waiting for a long letter from you.

I embrace you dearly.

Yours,
B

Third Letter, Sunday, 7 February 1943

My beloved Maurice,

We broke the record for letters this week. Fortunately, we're fine and it's nice to receive a letter every three days because it makes us feel like we're together. I told you in my last letter that I received the calcium boxes, 12 vials in total. I'll try to take them because even though I work and walk, I don't understand why I feel so agitated, among other things.

Regarding my personal details, I was told that these won't be necessary from the moment the permit is sent from Athens. Mr. Tiano, who is well known, can give them the details.

Today, I received your letter of 1 February in which you inform me of the steps you have taken. I trust Mr. Tiano because he likes me and he knows people. I'll go see Albert Gattegno[29] this afternoon to ask him for the letter. May God help the three of us. Last night I dreamt of you wearing the brown jacket I love, and you were very happy. I was in a good mood when I got up.

Home: Going down Misrahi Street toward Hirsch Hospital,[30] turn to the second street on the right, Deligiorgi [address: Deligiorgi, 33],[31] our house is four houses down; about ten steps further—the third door from Gouzios' house. Our home is on one floor, you enter through a courtyard, which is surrounded by flowers, climb five steps to the hall. Our room is opposite the door. [. . .] My bed is opposite Berto's bed, which has a bronze eagle with spread wings (toward Benaroya),[32] and next to a window overlooking a small terrace with four walls in the garden. During winter, it's the nest of meowing cats, in the summer the birds wake us up at 4 a.m. and at the fruit season at 2 a.m. with their quarrelling. We have a sofa in between the two beds and a small improvised table in the middle of the room with a square board that moves the moment we go near it. A brown cupboard in the corner for our clothes, a neighbor's chest and our two suitcases—one on top of the chest and another under the bed.

Mrs. Dona is always busy with her daughter, she commutes every day, she's never at home, and when she is, her husband works at home (by correspondence) and is always in a bad mood. Mrs. Dona's hair is already white and aged. Her brother works with her two sons.

Weather: Yesterday it rained a lot in the morning. I went to see about father's certificate,[33] we have to get it done at the community. I'll try to go. Tomorrow, Monday, I'm going to see Aunt Leah who doesn't trust doctors at all.

My son,[34] why doesn't the stupid lawyer pay you? The first of the month shouldn't be missed when it's time to pay, because afterwards he believes that it's already a fine.[35] Let me know when you get the shoes.

I went to Albert Gattegno's house in the afternoon to ask him for the recommendation letter. He kindly agreed to give it to me, but he told me that, as Sourianos couldn't do anything for him, he wondered how we could expect him to do it for us? However, if a letter giving references of good repute for you, Berto, and I is required, he will write one for us from all his heart. He told me that the letter will be ready tomorrow at 11 or 12 o'clock. I hope you succeed.

Meanwhile, I embrace you with all my heart. Your mother who loves you.

Neama

In the evening, I went to see Aunt Lea who is in a serious state. I'll go keep her company tomorrow morning. We're waiting for Henriette who'll be arriving late.

Tonight Berto and the neighbor are discussing the laws of marriage. He thinks he can unsettle him with his unorthodox ideas. He would have ended up in an insane asylum if you had also been there, especially because Berto would burst out laughing every time he was confused.

Letter from Berto, Tuesday, 9 February 1943

My dearest Maurice,

I would like to write you a long letter, but I am very busy with the sale of soap, which works very well. It looks like the polish will make me *lose*, because it does not sell and runs the risk of getting spoiled. If you need recipes, I prepare it by myself, and I know everything you need to know.

Even though the weather is rainy, we are thinking of organizing a big excursion one of these days. In addition, the friends of Angele want to organize a big party with decorations on the occasion of the mid-lent. *All* the friends of Mr. Scafra will be invited. It is going to be a family party, which will bring all of us together and spend a nice long evening. These days we have crazy preparations. How I regret that you are not here to have fun . . .

Attached I am sending you a sample of my jacket, so you get an idea of the color. The pants should be of the same color, more or less. The cotton is checkered. For the moment, *it is not urgent*. I will need the pants for spring. For now, the raincoat is enough.

And this, as a means of a conclusion, to show you that my spirits are well. Mother is doing well. Gina as well.

I kiss you very affectionately,
Your Berto

Fourth Letter, Thursday, 11 February 1943

My beloved Maurice,

I received your letter of 4 February and the copy of the procedures required for my permit this morning.[36] As soon as you receive this letter, please hurry so I can get the permit as soon as possible because the weather has changed abruptly from snow to rain, and the persistent humidity has aggravated my rheumatism. The doctors are in despair because my legs might get paralyzed for good. I have no other choice but to rely on you, with the few means that you have, and on Mr. T., to save me from this disease in time. I saw Albert's father this morning, and he agrees with the change of climate the soonest.

I sent you the letter for the medicine you asked for. I hope Esther's husband will do everything in his power to put an end to this forsaken situation.

Excursions and walks were in full swing last week because the weather was milder. Tina sends you her greetings.

Alice has shown herself to be at the height of her kindness. She invites us to her home in the evenings because her house is warmer and ideal for poultices and my massages. She even invites us to stay with her for good. We'll never be able to repay her for her kindness.

Aunt Lea is a bit better. She has a tumor in her liver, and Alice goes to see her every day.

Dora came to see me straightaway in order to go to the doctor because she has the same type of rheumatism as me, and she needs to move to a cleaner house.

Jeannette has started to walk taking small steps.

Dingas sent me the shots.

Foti's friends are very attentive toward us. We hope we'll be able to repay them for their kindness.

The tenant didn't come for the small room. We're waiting for the whole family to come live with us—the owner's sister and her husband, her son and two daughters, and the stepmother.

I pray to God that you succeed, and that I manage to think more clearly. Berto will write to you.

I embrace you with all my heart.

Your mother,
Neama

I hope to hear from you right away.

Letter from Berto, Saturday, 1[3] February 1943

My dear Maurice,

Today, Mitzo's brother will go find Tagara, and from there he'll go see Tzeblas' brother. I'll send you more details in due course.

At home, mother is fine. Alice is in a very bad state. That's why Mitzo's brother will call the doctor.

I'm in a great hurry. I'll write to you later.

I embrace you fondly,
Berthy

Fifth Letter, Saturday, 20 February 1943

My beloved Maurice,

Yesterday, I received the wire[37] in which you tell me you are well, and it made me feel better. I can't possibly describe to you what I've been going through. I had written a letter to you and it was ready to be sent. I didn't send it though as I was waiting for news of your health. Fortunately, you are well—just as I had wished.

I slept well and ate well yesterday evening.

Gina came to see me at 2 o'clock. We took a short walk, and then we went to see Mrs. Tabaki, who consoles me. Now that she's living at the Avayous' accountant's place, she's closer to home.

I received the remittance of 20,000 this morning. I had borrowed two thousand because I didn't have a cent.

I have a lot of bread because all the food portions[38] are intact. You just need to be hungry enough to eat them.

This morning, we went with Gina to Dora's, to Lisa's and her mother's, and we took a short walk on the seafront. On the way there, I saw the postman and he handed me two letters from you. I'm waiting, and

I think you'll succeed in obtaining my permit, as long as I'm successful here, too. I would be very happy then.

I rented out my room to Elda Nahmias this morning, and I'll live in the glass patio[39] where the owner will also place his mother-in-law. Elda's husband is very talkative, so we manage to forget about our problems for a little while. They have a baby who murmurs all day.

I went to see the Broudos to ask about their health the day before yesterday. Uncle Menachem resides next to Lisa.[40]

The weather is very nice, and there are plenty of distractions. If I'm in a good mood one day, it would be fun to see Jousse with the new tenant. One of them is religious and the other one is disbelieving and spiritual.

Luckily, as I slept well today, I'm calm. I took the opportunity to write to you and give you the impression that I'm in good spirits while waiting for the final answer for the permit.

Mrs. Levy behaved impeccably toward me these past days. The parents have kept to themselves.

I found Davico for the shots, and he'll come tomorrow.

It will be difficult to post this letter, so the new neighbor will take it on foot. He's very helpful. I have behaved well toward them, but they don't know how to act toward me.

According to Elda, her sister Alice, who is married to Joseph Modiano[41] from Cavalla,[42] can be of great assistance to you. She lives at 157 Janni Drossopoulo Patission Street.

Daisy and her husband, that imbecile who created problems for me and whom I had to rebuke, send you their greetings.

I eagerly await your letter. I wish you success in your work so that you don't get bored. Give my regards to Cantas, and tell him that the time has come for me to see the extent of his friendship toward me.

I embrace you with all my heart.

Your mother who is thinking of you and waiting to see you again,
Neama

Sixth Letter, Sunday, 21 February 1943

My dear Maurice,

Last night, I received your wire about the permit. I might go see if it has arrived tomorrow, but I doubt it because I've been told it's very difficult. It would be a miracle if I were to succeed.

Joseph Molho—the son of our tenant Mr. Molho—is very resourceful. Let's see whether he'll be able to do something.

We declared the room with him this morning. Everyone has to do it.

I received the 20,000 drachmas and I have it in safekeeping now. I might need more to finish my work.

I pray to the good God to answer my prayers, and that I'll be able see you again in good health.

I await your letter. I embrace you with all my heart.

Your mother,
Neama

Tina and Gina send you their greetings.

Seventh Letter, Thursday, 18 March 1943

My dear Maurice,

The permit arrived yesterday. I did everything I could with the help of Albert's father who lives near me. He told me he'd do his best, but he doesn't think he'll succeed. I expect an answer today. I'm at the height of my despair because we'll be expedited any day now—from one moment to the next—and only God can save us. I can't tell you what's happening—it's indescribable. May God perform a miracle.

I received the money right away. It no longer has any value for me because what will I do without you?

May God help us. Be well. I wish what a mother's heart would wish for her beloved children. God save us!

Gina is fine.

We're ready and fully prepared. Only God can save us.

I embrace you with all my strength, my heart, my darlings, my beloved. God have mercy on us.

Your mother who only thinks of her children.

Neama

May God perform a miracle so that I see you again.

I'll write again if I have any news.

They just announced that the departure will be postponed[43] for a few days, but nobody wants to believe it.[44]

Two convoys have already left.[45]

Eighth Letter, Friday, 19 March 1943

My dear Maurice,

The permit has arrived. The Italian Consul allows the sick to leave, but the German authorities don't. According to Albert's father, the Consul is taking steps in Athens to obtain the permit from here, because the patient is very ill and must be operated in time.

I sent you two telegrams, and I'll call you on the phone.[46] Albert's father tells me that you're doing all you can to hasten things on time. I hope you succeed—may God help you.

I sent you a letter. I doubt you received it because Tina sent it. Get to work as soon as possible.

I embrace you and Berto with all my heart.
Your mother who thinks of you.
Neama

I just received your letters. I can't answer them. I don't know what to write given the state the patient is in—with a temperature of 40, and I don't know if we can save her.

Ninth Letter, Thursday, 24 March 1943

My dear children,

I would have waited for your letter before writing to you, but as the sick woman is a bit better, I decided to write now. It is 9 o'clock in the evening.

It started snowing yesterday morning at 4 a.m., and we're shivering from the cold. We hope the weather will change tonight because sometimes it's windy and sometimes it snows.

I went to see Albert's father in the morning to finally receive a negative answer. Can't Kantas' friend be of any help?

Many people manage to find a way to send a parcel. When we were busy during Purim,[47] and in order to make to me happy, Yousse brought me eight cakes from the pastry shop opposite Liza's husband's place to send with the parcel, but I haven't been able to send it yet.

Can't Alice's and Kantas' friend do something for me?

Gina is fine. She came to me to see last night.

Many kisses.

Your mother,
Neama

Why doesn't Berto write?

Tenth Letter, Saturday, 27 March 1943

My dearest children,

Today I received two letters from you, Maurice, one through the postman, the other through Gina and Pajaitis' daughter. I was worried because I hadn't heard from Aleco.[48] I send you letters even though I'm absentminded, but you don't receive all of them.

Nothing can describe what we're going through. We live with Alice's disease all day and all night. We're waiting for the fatal blow from one moment to the next.

This morning, I went to get a permission to be escorted at the Consulate.[49] I took the permit to the Consul who showed interest in me, but he can't do anything about the second signature, only God can. I struggle in every way possible only to end up with nothing. May God, who sees my anguish, have mercy on us.

For the chemist's nameday celebration, I offered him the overcoat, Aleco's suit, and grandmother's gift. I haven't been able to see him for a month.

Gina came by this evening and we read the letters together. Your letters are a great consolation to me, but the illness is very serious. We are at the patient's bedside all night. I think every letter I write is the last. The disease has developed serious complications. My only consolation is seeing Gina for fifteen minutes in the evening.

This evening, despite the fatigue, I went to see Aunt Lea who thinks she sees her salvation when I go to her house. She is condemned to die, and even though I lavish her with attention, she's dying of hunger; and her son has yet to write her a letter even in this state. He mustn't have a clear conscience because she looks like a skeleton in bed, and I'm the only one who takes care of her. I'm the only one who combs her hair and keeps her company. Albert doesn't have a cent.

I believe with this good deed,[50] God will let me see my children again, my only happiness, my only reason for living. She blesses me, may God hear the prayers and the blessings. My soul is with God day and night so that he helps me stay close to you.

Send me as many letters as possible because I have no other aspiration in life, besides my children.

Vassil comes to see me twice a week. He alleviates much of my pain.

Gina will write to you. My registration number is 6152.

Take care and may God answer my prayer. I embrace you with all my love.

Your mother who adores you,
Neama

Eleventh Letter, Thursday, 1 April 1943

My dearest,

I received the postcard and the letter addressed to Miki through Gina. She brought it this morning and stayed for half an hour because she didn't have much to do besides housework.

Your letter touched me very much, my dear children. May God, who sees how anxious we have become, save us in time because the problems and the panic we feel have made us dumb. We look at each other, we stay silent, we don't exchange one word, we just point toward God.

We were calmer the past two days. We hope that Providence will take care of us because we're picking our brains night and day to no avail.

I try to go to bed early in order to sleep in the evening. I sleep for two hours, and I then wake up with a start. What will become of me without my children? When will I see them again? Where is this "unknown" that I will be sent to alone? My brain is overtired, and the nightmare haunts me so much that I feel my head is made of cement and that my thoughts can't find a way out. It's true that I'm not the only one suffering, but I've been bled dry for a long time, and our separation has worn me down.

If God wants me to see you again, He'll give me the strength to resist, to have you near me, to feel that I'm surrounded by the affection that was the only joy in my life.

My neighbor tries to cheer me up despite his own worries, but I feel so alone in this storm that I nearly did something crazy the other day. Although it may seem strange, and it will make you smile, I nearly married an old man who was paralyzed in order to change nationality. However, common sense reminded me that I would be leaving one difficult situation[51] for another inextricable one, and there were already five contenders willing to take care of him.

Hundreds of young people get married ten at a time just to have a companion. They are wed by the rabbi without a dowry, only a backpack. Mr. Yeni wed his son to a young girl who could become his friend.

We're all at home by 4:30 in the evening. Gina stays with us for fifteen minutes.

May God protect you from all evil, and I expect [to] hear from you very often. I don't think God will test us anymore. A moment of calm gives me hope, like today that the weather was nice.

The Avayous have moved close to us, at Edmond Rostand Street,[52] but I'm not in the right frame of mind to go see them.

Vital hardly comes home. Mario is unemployed and in dire straits. He wanted to get married.

We think of others during calm moments. I hope to God that these moments become permanent so that our souls and our minds get some rest.

I kiss you with all my heart.

Your mother,
Neama

[Written around the sides of the letter]

Check with a friend whether you can send the parcel[53] from here.

Mr. Levy reads psalms at home with all his friends. Our neighbor Youssi sends you his regards and prays to God that he'll be able to eat apricots in autumn now that the trees have bloomed. May God watch over us.

Twelfth Letter, Sunday, 4 April 1943

My dearest Maurice and Berto,[54]

I received Berto's letter today, and I don't know when I'll receive another one.

Despite having to live in agony all day and night like inmates awaiting their death sentence, I'm writing to you to help you calm down a little. We were briefly under the illusion that we could run away from these terrible times. But things are rapidly gathering pace. My fatal moment will arrive in a few days or hours, too.

My dear children, despite keeping my self-control so as not to grieve you, I see that my last hours have arrived. Nothing can console me in the knowledge that I'll be separated for good from my dear children, my loved ones whom I so desperately want to see, those by my side, and in my last days—the only joys of my life. I haven't enjoyed a single day of my stay here because we've been separated. I had foreseen all this and I wanted to leave in time, but I met all sorts of obstacles. I don't know if I'll be able to live with the nostalgia, deprivation, and misery.

God, who sees my tears, have mercy and protect you. Live happily if you can. May God protect you from all evil—this is my prayer every night.

Nothing can depict the tragedy that is taking place here. What hope is there in continuing to resist so much? I was expecting to see you at any moment, and now I must run with my backpack toward the unknown without anyone to protect me?

Don't forget me, my dear children, my beloved ones, my only reason for living. If God could only give me hope that I'll see you again, kiss you again, see your eyes again—eyes for which I spent my youth always hoping to spend happy days with. If I ever hear from you, or you from me, who knows whether God will protect me. I'll go to the office or to Tiano's. We no longer know when God will reunite us.

Think of me at all times, I suffer a lot. I foresaw these moments, and I thought we'd be together. May God have mercy on me so that I don't fall ill, so that they don't exterminate me. Because what we see is not very encouraging.

The coat, fabric, gift from grandmother, and the other small things are at the chemist's, the suitcase with all my and Berto's belongings are with Vanguelo, the neighbor who lives next to our house at Menelaos Karamihail, 60 Miaoulis Street.

We lie fully clothed because we need to wake up at midnight.

Gina received the letter.

I can't continue writing any longer, be well and in good health. May God help you and that I don't die before seeing you both again.

I embrace you with my heart that is dying for you.

Your very unfortunate mother,
Neama

[Written on the side]

I embrace you once again, my sons Maurice and Berto.

I don't know if I'll end up with Gina at the last moment, because we don't know how they will block us. In any case, God will help me if he wants me to see you again.

Thirteenth Letter, Thursday, 8 April 1943

My dear Maurice and Berto,[55]

I received your letter, and it's clear to me that you don't know what we're going through. Only in stories or at the cinema can you see scenes similar to what we're going through this week.

We have sat in bed fully dressed for two nights waiting for someone to knock on the door, wake us up and take us. Everyone is selling one's personal belongings in the streets and buying things to eat. We waste money as if it were water, we throw money out of the window. Personal belongings are distributed to whoever is interested. The crying, the groaning, the tragedies cannot be described.

The day before yesterday, the pharmacist's daughter came to see me, and I asked her to tell her father that I wanted to pay him a long visit and then sleep. He refused. His daughter came over again today and brought me a small jar of marmalade along with a small brioche.[56] She apologized for his refusal.

Pazaitis' wife comes by three times a day to ask Gina and me for some personal belongings. We gave her some, but nothing of mine. I gave her the suitcase with my and Berto's belongings. I took them from Vanguelo's other neighbor because I thought they would be safer at Pazaitis' place.

The streets are packed with people trying to catch and steal people's belongings like a bunch of hyenas circling a dead horse. Jousse sold three-fourths, and the only thing Daisy does is cry all day seeing merchants entering her home. A true flea market.

It's like living your worst nightmare, day and night, in indescribable anguish. Everyone has a cart ready outside one's door. Ida bought one for 120,000 to transport her belongings and the baby. We're wondering what to do with Aunt Lea who'll succumb in the middle of the journey to the station. Gina gave all of her hats and gloves to Soula, the pharmacist.

We were notified last night that we would be leaving this morning. Now, we don't know what day of the week we'll leave. If we don't leave tomorrow, we have until the 15th to leave.

I don't sleep at night, and my only thoughts are of you, that this terrible wind doesn't blow in your direction as well. May God bless you, my dear children, as my thoughts will become even more muddled once I no longer know where you are.

Pay an extended visit to Gouzios and give him my regards. He's done so much for you, and will continue to do so.

We'll try to be together with Gina, but we don't know how they will block us. In any case, we think we'll be together or with Ida who is in the same block as us. My bag was ready, but it wasn't solid enough, and I couldn't lift it. Gina helped me pack another bag today.

She tries to make me think positively, but I can't get over not knowing when I'll see you again. God has become deaf to my prayers, but I still pray to him.

The weather here helps with the melancholia. If the weather changes where you are, as it is spring, beware of the cold because the changes in temperature are very unhealthy. Be well and always stay together.

Try to find me with Gina because the thought of you not knowing where we are is driving me crazy. Gina is sometimes in a better mood, and she lifts my spirits a little. May God help us, and reunite us all in good health.

I embrace you with all my heart and soul, my dearest children. May the good Lord have mercy on the innocent who aspire only to simple family pleasures. May God watch over you and keep you from all evil.

Your mother only has one thought on her mind: to see her children well. Gina will write to you.

Your mother,
Neama

[Written on the side]

Madame Avayou is near us. I saw her last night. Don't ask.[57]

If we can, I'll use all the addresses. Theo's mother left. Liza and Aunt Mery[58] as well. Foti's friends are also waiting to celebrate Easter.[59]

Mario sold Beno's belongings, and he also wanted to get married. He didn't manage to. His brother will also leave.

I'm doing well despite all these worries. Procop lent me 50 thousand drachmas for the travel expenses. Don't send money.

Letter from Maurice That Was Returned, Friday, 9 April 1943

My dear Mouca,

I think of you all the time. I think of you so often and so intensely that I might have found it superfluous to write to you had it not been for the fact that receiving a letter helps a person feel less lonely during these times.

The news I hear is contradictory, to say the least. There are times when I hope that a middle-ground solution can be found in time, despite the agony we're going through, and that the worst will be avoided for an indefinite period of time. We'll see what we'll do then, as long as you're with us, of course. As for your future actions, I have no doubt that you'll have the energy and the will to adapt to the circumstances.

In any case, act as you please and avoid getting bogged down by tiny details and their future consequences, and don't let yourself go. There is still some considerable hope. Mouca, I hug you and bid you farewell.

Lovingly,
Your m.

Kiss Gina on my behalf.

Fourteenth Letter, Saturday, 10 April 1943

Vital is responsible for sending off the refugees. He's at home only two days per week. As a Jewish civilian guard, he'll be the last to leave.

The four families are in two rooms without beds and without clothes.

Renée is trying to get all the paperwork done in order to get married. The day before yesterday, Mario got married at Beth Saul[60] all alone, and they slept on the floor planks.

Mery and Victoria are together. Mario's brother can't get married, she is an Italian subject.

Margot Levy's[61] fiancé was taken away right before they were supposed to get married. Just imagine the state she's in.

Eugenie and her mother left yesterday.

Last night, we got into bed fully dressed and we were ready. We're still here. We don't know whether we'll have to relive this agony again tomorrow.

It rained a lot yesterday. Today it's very cold. The wind is blowing violently, and it's snowing a little.

Does Aleco have a job? He should be careful of the changes in weather. Especially these days when it rains.

Dario Cuenca left with his sick wife.[62]

Everyone feels sorry for me, but they can't help me. May God help us and reunite us unharmed as soon as possible.

I embrace you with all my soul, my dear children and may God watch over you.

Your mother,
Neama

Letter from Berto That Was Returned, Tuesday, 13 April 1943

I was right to write to you about Angelu.

My beloved Mouca,[63]

I haven't heard from you for a long time, and I'm worried. Fortunately, my dear Mouca, Gina wrote to me at length about you in her letter of 6 April.

At the moment, I'm still taking my exams. I hope Gadol[64] will do something for us.

It would be pointless to describe to you the state I've been in since Alice's illness because I can imagine how anxious you must feel with your own dear little girl being so sick. I'm speaking frankly to you without hiding anything. There are times when her temperature is very high. I despair, but still have hope, great hope, and faith in God.

I repeat the same thing on purpose in every letter I write to make you understand that you should never lose hope even if Alice is obliged to stay in a hospital for some time. Like you, I know what a bitter experience it is.

You'll see better days, my Mouca darling, and rest assured that Alice will be cured.

So hold on Mouca, and together with my little Gina, always love and stay close to each other. I embrace you with all my heart.

Your Nico[65]

Mitzo will write tomorrow.

Letter from Maurice That Was Returned, Tuesday, 13 April 1943

My very dear Mouca,

Neither today did we receive a letter from your part. Naturally, this does not alleviate our concerns. I don't believe it will be possible to worry even more given the acuteness of our anxiety. I try to find an explanation for your silence and I ask myself if it is not the suspension of airmail service that is the cause of your prolonged silence. Of course, I do not have any illusions on the state of your health and the state of your nervous system. Due to the distance that separates us, I am angry at not being able to give you even the illusion of protection by hugging you tightly in my arms.

From your side also, I don't doubt that you must also be very worried about our dear Emma-Gina. Her state, although stable, leaves a lot of hope. At least, this is the opinion of the chief doctor who examined her at home and who told us that the operation could be avoided. With the time that is running out and the scarcity of medicines and money, this will be truly a grace.

Yesterday evening, speaking about you as usual, to change a bit the air and the surroundings, we thought that you can go spend the Easter holidays at my old friend's, the dentist Nico Palanghias, in his property in the village close to Inglis.[66] I will tell his brother, Argyri, to come and look for you, if necessary, in case you hesitate for one reason or another.

I will write you again tomorrow. I hope that this letter does not take a century to get to you and that it finds you a bit better. And you, write to me every time that you can and don't forget to tell me if you need money and what amount you want me to send you.

So long my dear Mouca,

Lovingly,
Your m.

Notes

1. Letter was written on a transparent paper. Neama Cazes' first three letters were sent together with a letter from Berto. After 20 February, when Berto had left for Athens, Neama Cazes sent the letters on her own.
2. Religious Jews are not allowed to cook on Saturday.
3. Greek Orthodox Christians cross themselves as a sign of belief to God.
4. Referring to Karagöz and Hadjivat, lead characters from a traditional Turkish shadow play.
5. Street at the eastern part of Thessaloniki.
6. Traditional Sephardic pastry.
7. She refers to a permit required to travel to Athens.
8. Traditional Sephardic cookies in the shape of a ring.
9. Expression in Judeo-Spanish.
10. Nonperishable goods, such as shoe polish and soap, apart from their normal usage, also had safekeeping value during the war.
11. Mimicking the selling phrase in Greek, written in Greek script.
12. Carob was a widespread food during the war.
13. Word in Judeo-Spanish.
14. Word in Greek script.
15. This recalls the 1935 French song, "Tout va très bien madame la marquise," which ironically claims that everything goes well at a time when big disasters are taking place.
16. He refers to the last transparent paper she used.
17. Expression in Greek script.

18. An Ottoman measure of mass, around 1.3 kilograms.
19. Greek word written in Latin script.
20. Expression in Judeo-Spanish.
21. The reduced fare was 100 drachmas, so this is the cost for a return ticket.
22. An area of the seafront of Thessaloniki in the eastern part of town.
23. Expression in Judeo-Spanish.
24. Lucie Angel, wife of Isaac, née Beja was born in 1896. All the family survived in Athens.
25. Expression in Greek script.
26. Expression in Greek script.
27. Expression in Greek script.
28. The central market in downtown Thessaloniki.
29. Albert Gattegno provided a reference letter for Maurice Cazes addressed to Henri Asseo in Athens dated 8 February 1943.
30. The main Jewish hospital of Thessaloniki, named after the benefactor Baron Hirsch.
31. In the eastern part of Thessaloniki.
32. Avraam Benaroya was a prominent Socialist leader in Thessaloniki, founder of the workers' party, "Socialist Workers' Federation." He survived the war, imprisoned in a German camp and after the war migrated to Israel.
33. Greek word in Latin script.
34. Phrase in Judeo-Spanish.
35. Word in Turkish.
36. On 8 February 1943, Maurice Cazes wrote a letter to the Italian Representation in Athens, asking for his mother and brother to be allowed to travel to Athens.
37. Presumably the telegraph informing her that Berto had arrived safely in Athens.
38. Greek word written in Latin script.
39. Word from Turkish.
40. Elise (Lisa) Salem, daughter of Menachem and Mery Cazes, first cousin of Maurice and Alberto Cazes. She was married to David Salem, furniture maker. They were both deported and murdered in Auschwitz, together with their three-year-old daughter Renée and the rest of their families. Mery Cazes was the sister of Albert Gattegno, who is mentioned in the letters. Before they were deported, Elise and David Salem stayed with Isaac Nahmias, the business partner of Albert Gattegno. Berto Cazes was very close to David Salem, and he learned furniture making from him.
41. Joseph Modiano, of Elias, was born in 1903. His wife was called Alice and his son Maurice. He was an employee and resided in Athens in 1946.
42. Kavala is a Greek city east of Thessaloniki.
43. Greek word written in Latin script.
44. Different rumors circulated in the ghetto about a possible postponement of the deportations: a change of German policy, a successful intervention by the Greek authorities, a German loss in the battlefield, or even the entry of Turkey to the war at the side of the Allies. Molho and Nehama, *In Memoriam*, 113.
45. The first train departed on 15 March 1943.
46. Greek expression translated in French.
47. Purim is a Jewish festival that commemorates the saving of the Jewish people in ancient Persia, as recounted in the Book of Esther. Customs include wearing masks and costumes, public celebrations and parades, and drinking wine or other alcoholic beverages. Purim that year was on Sunday, 21 March 1943.
48. A Greek-sounding name for Alberto-Berto.
49. The Italian Consulate was located on 20 Vassilissis Olgas avenue, close to the home of Ms. Cazes.
50. Word in Hebrew.

51. A word in Turkish, also used in Greek.
52. A street in the eastern part of Thessaloniki.
53. Greek word in Latin script.
54. The letter was dated the month of March by mistake.
55. The letter was dated the month of March by mistake.
56. A typical sweet pastry of Thessaloniki.
57. Greek phrase written in Latin script.
58. Mery Cazes née Gattegno was the wife of Menahem, brother of Yehuda Cazes, Neama Cazes' husband. Mery was the sister of Albert Gattegno, who is mentioned in the letters.
59. The Greek Orthodox Easter was on 12 April that year.
60. The main synagogue of Thessaloniki before the war, it was destroyed in 1943. It was founded in 1898 by Fakima Modiano, in memory of her husband Saul, a leading businessman, banker and philanthropist. It was located in the eastern part of Thessaloniki.
61. Margot Levy, daughter of Moses and Anna, was born in 1923. She was a victim of the Holocaust.
62. Dario Cuenca, of Levi and Sohoula, was born in 1907. His wife was Ester-Rina Salem, both victims of the Holocaust.
63. Returned envelop bearing a censor's stamp.
64. Refers to God. *Gadol* in Hebrew means "big."
65. The fake name Berto assumed while hiding in Athens.
66. It refers to the village of Nea Achialos, in Thessaloniki. It used to be called "Inglis," because the land belonged to an Englishman who was killed by the Turks.

Bibliography

Algava, Andreas. *600 Days in Hiding: A Jewish Family in Nazi-Occupied Thessaloniki, Greece*. Bellingham, WA: For Passion Publishing Company, 2018.

Apostolou, Andrew. "'The Exception of Salonika': Bystanders and Collaborators in Northern Greece." *Holocaust and Genocide Studies* 14, no. 2 (Autumn 2000): 165–96.

Asser Pardo, Rozina. *548 Days with Another Name: Salonika 1943; A Child's Diary, An Adult's Memories of War*. New York: Bloch Publishing Company, 2006.

Avloniti, Evangelia. "The Holocaust and the Story of Greek Jews in Publishing." *Publishing Perspectives*, 12 June 2015. Retrieved 1 August 2020 from http://publishingperspectives.com/2015/06/the-holocaust-and-the-story-of-greek-jews-in-publishing.

Bacharach, Zwi. *Last Letters from the Shoah*. Jerusalem: Yad Vashem and Devora Publishing, 2004.

Benveniste, Rika. "H Istoriografia gia to Olokautoma stin Ellada" [The historiography on the Holocaust in Greece]. *Sychrona Themata* 76–77 (January–July 2001): 104–9.

———. "The Coming Out of Jewish History in Greece." Atelier international de recherche sur les usages publics du passé, 27 January 2001. Retrieved 1 August 2020 from http://anciensiteusagespublicsdupasse.ehess.fr/index.php?id=130.

Bowman, Steven, ed. *The Holocaust in Salonika: Eyewitness Accounts*. New York: Bloch, 2002.

Bunis, David. "Salonika: World Center of Popular Judezmism." In *Judeo-Espaniol: A Jewish Language in Search of Its People*, edited by Raphael Gatenio, 75–84. Thessaloniki: Jewish Community of Thessaloniki and Ets Ahaim Foundation, 2002.

Carpi, Daniel, ed. *Italian Diplomatic Documents on the History of the Holocaust in Greece (1941–1943)*. Tel Aviv: Diaspora Research Institute, The Chair in the History and Culture of the Jews of Salonika and Greece, Tel Aviv University, 1999.

Clogg, Richard, ed. *Bearing Gifts to Greeks: Humanitarian Aid to Greece in the 1940s*. Basingstoke: Palgrave-Macmillan, 2007.

Czech, Danuta. *Auschwitz Chronicle 1939–1945*. New York: I. B. Tauris & Co Ltd Publishers, 1990.

Dodos, Dimosthenis. *Oi Ebraioi tis Thessalonikis stis Ekloges tou Ellinikou Kratous 1915–1936* [The Jews of Thessaloniki in the elections of the Greek State 1915–1936]. Athens: Savalas, 2005.

Dordanas, Stratos. "'O Ehthros me tin Pena': H Diki ton Dimosiografon tis Neas Evropis kai Apogevmatinis" [The enemy with the pen: The trial of the journalists of Nea Evropi and Apogevmatini]. In *Ethniki Antistasi 1941–1944: O Paranomos Typos sti Boreia Ellada* [National resistance 1941–1944: The illegal press in Northern Greece] edited by Giannis Kotsifos, 150–63. Thessaloniki: Educational Foundation of the Union of Journalists of Daily Newspapers of Macedonia-Thrace, 2009.

———. "Exontosi kai Leilasia: H Ypiresia Diaxeiriseos Israilitikon Periousion" [Extermination and plunder: Agency for the custody of Jewish properties]. In *To Olokautoma sta Balkania* [The Holocaust in the Balkans], edited by Giorgos Antoniou, Stratos Dordanas, Nikos Zaikos, Nikos Marantzidis, 331–52. Thessaloniki: Epikentro, 2011.

Dublon-Knebel, Irith, ed. *German Foreign Office Documents on the Holocaust in Greece (1937–1944)*. Tel Aviv: Tel Aviv University, 2007.

Fleischer, Hagen. *Stemma kai Svastiga: H Ellada tis Katohis kai tis Antistasis 1941–1944* [Crown and swastika: Greece during the occupation and the resistance]. Athens: Papazisis, 1995.

Ginio, Eyal. "'Learning the Beautiful Language of Homer': Judeo-Spanish Speaking Jews and the Greek Language and Culture between the Wars." *Jewish History* 16, no. 3 (2002): 235–62.

Hadar, Gila. "Marriage as Survival Strategy on the Eve of the Deportation, Salonika 1943." International symposium, "The Holocaust of Greek Jewry," University of Haifa, December 2002.

———. "Space and Time in Salonika on the Eve of World War II and the Expulsion and Extermination of Salonika Jewry (1939–1945)." *Yelkut Moreshet* 4 (2006): 65–72.

Handrinos, Georgios. "Ta 'Trena tou Thanatou': Apo ti Thessaloniki sto Auschwitz" [The "trains of death": From Thessaloniki to Auschwitz]. *Sidirotrohia* 43–44 (December 2013): 18–32.

Hekimoglou, Evanghelos. "The Exact Location of the Ghettos in Thessaloniki, 1943." Unpublished report written for the Jewish Community of Thessaloniki, 30 July 2013. Retrieved 1 August 2020 from https://www.academia.edu/10614219/The_exact_location_of_the_Ghettos_in_Thessaloniki_1943.

Helger, Bengt, *Ravitaillement de la Grèce pendant l'Occupation 1941–1944 et pendant les premiers cinq mois après la Libération: Rapport final de la Commission de Gestion pour les Secours en Grèce sous les auspices du Comité International de la Croix-Rouge*. Athens: Imprimerie de la "Société Hellénique d'Editions" S.A., 1949.

Hionidou, Violetta. *Famine and Death in Occupied Greece, 1941–1944*. Cambridge: Cambridge University Press, 2006.

Ingram, Janine. *Unaccounted For*. London, 1989.

Kavala, Maria, "Epiviosi Biologiki kai Pneumatiki" [Survival biological and spiritual]. In *O Foros tou Aimatos stin Katoxiki Thessaloniki: Xeni Kyriarhia—Antistasi kai Epiviosi* [The burden of blood in occupied Thessaloniki: Foreign domination—resistance and survival], edited by Basil Gounaris and Petros Papapolyviou, 16–23. Thessaloniki: Paratiritis, 2001.

———. "H Thessaloniki sti Germaniki Katoxi (1941–1944): Koinonia, Oikonomia, Diogmos Ebraion" [Thessaloniki during the German occupation (1941–1944): Society, economy, persecution of Jews]. PhD diss., University of Crete, Rethymno, 2009.

Kralova, Katerina, Marija Vulesica, and Giorgos Antoniou, eds. *Jewish Life in Southeast Europe: Diverse Perspectives on the Holocaust and Beyond*. London: Routledge, 2019.

Margaritis, Giorgios. *Anepithimitoi Sympatriotes: Stoiheia gia tin Katastrofi ton Meionotiton tis Elladas; Ebraioi, Tsamides* [Unwanted compatriots: Data on the destruction of the minorities of Greece; Jews and Chams]. Athens: Bibliorama, 2005.

Mazower, Mark. *Salonica: City of Ghosts*. New York: Alfred A. Knopf, 2005.

Merten, Max. "Testimony to the Eichmann Trial." Nizkor Project, Part 1 of 3, 7 May 1961. Retrieved 1 August 2020 from http://www.nizkor.com/hweb/people/e/eichmann-adolf/transcripts/Testimony-Abroad/Max_Merten-01.html.

Molho, Anthony. "Introduction." *Jewish History* 28, nos. 3–4 (December 2014): 249–59.

Molho, Michael, and Joseph Nehama. *In Memoriam: Afieroma eis tin Mnimin ton Israiliton Thymaton toy Nazismou en Elladi* [In memoriam: Dedication to the memory of the Jewish victims of Nazism in Greece]. Thessaloniki: Jewish Community of Thessaloniki, 1974.

Molho, Rena. "Education in the Jewish Community of Thessaloniki in the Beginning of the 20th Century." *Balkan Studies* 34, no. 2 (1993): 259–69.

———. *Oi Ebraioi tis Thessalonikis 1856–1919: Mia Idiaiteri Koinotita* [The Jews of Thessaloniki: A particular community]. Athens: Themelio, 2001.

———. *To Olokautoma ton Ellinon Ebraion: Meletes Istorias kai Mnimis* [The Holocaust of the Greek Jews: Studies of history and memory]. Athens: Pataki, 2014.

Naar, Devin. *Jewish Salonica: Between the Ottoman Empire and Modern Greece*. Stanford, CA: Stanford University Press, 2016.

Nehama, Joseph. *Istoria ton Israiliton tis Salonikis* [History of the Jews of Thessaloniki]. Vol. 3. Thessaloniki: Jewish Community of Thessaloniki and University Studio Press, 2000.

Patrikiou, Alexandra. "Mia 'Nea' Istoriki Periodos ypo Sygrotisi: Opseis tou Dimosiou Logou ton Efimeridon Nea Evropi kai Apogevmatini stin Katohiki Thessaloniki [A 'new' historical period under creation: Types of the public speech of the newspapers Nea Evropi and Apogevmatini in occupied Thessaloniki]. In *Ethniki Antistasi 1941–1944: O Paranomos Typos sti Boreia*

Ellada [National resistance 1941–1944: The illegal press in Northern Greece], edited by Giannis Kotsifos, 138–49. Thessaloniki: Educational Foundation of the Union of Journalists of Daily Newspapers of Macedonia-Thrace, 2009.

Ritzaleos, Vasilis. "H Elliniki Orthodoxi Ekklisia tis Thessalonikis kai to Olokautoma" [The Greek Orthodox Church of Thessaloniki and the Holocaust]. In *To Olokautoma sta Balkania* [The Holocaust in the Balkans], edited by Giorgos Antoniou, Stratos Dordanas, Nikos Zaikos, Nikos Marantzidis, 295–330. Thessaloniki: Epikentro, 2011.

Saltiel, Leon. "Voices from the Ghetto of Thessaloniki: Mother-Son Correspondence as a Source of Jewish Everyday Life under Persecution." *Journal of Southeast European and Black Sea Studies* 17, no. 2 (June 2017): 203–22.

———, ed. *"Mi Me Xehasete": Treis Ebraies Miteres Grafoun stous Gious tous apo to Ghetto tis Thessalonikis* ["Do not forget me": Three Jewish mothers write to their sons from the ghetto of Thessaloniki]. Athens: Alexandria, 2018.

———. *The Holocaust in Thessaloniki: Reactions to the Anti-Jewish Persecution 1942–1943*. New York: Routledge, 2020.

Stavroulakis, Nikos. "Letters from Salonika, 1943." *Newsletter of the Jewish Museum of Greece* 33, no. 1 (Autumn 1992): 4–8.

Tahvonen, Eryk Emil. "Perpetrators and Possibilities: Holocaust Diaries, Resistance, and the Crisis of Imagination." Master's thesis, Georgia State University, Atlanta, 2006.

Tsironis, Theodosis, "Onomatothesies kai Metonomasies Odon tis Thessalonikis me Israilitika Onomata" [Naming and renaming of Thessaloniki's streets bearing Jewish names]. *Thessaloniki: Scientific Yearbook of the Center of History of the Municipality of Thessaloniki* 9 (2017): 183–204.

United States Holocaust Memorial Museum. *Encyclopedia of Camps and Ghettos, 1933–1945*. Vol. 2: *Ghettos in German-Occupied Eastern Europe*. Edited by G. P. Megargee. Bloomington: Indiana University Press and the United States Holocaust Memorial Museum, 2009.

Varon-Vassard, Odette. "H Genoktonia ton Ellinon Ebraion (1943–1944) kai i Apotyposi tis: Martyries, Logotehnia kai Istoriografia" [The genocide of Greek Jews (1943–1944) and its depiction: Testimonies, literature and historiography]. In *H Anadysi mias Dyskolis Mnimis: Keimena gia ti Genoktonia ton Ebraion* [The emergence of a difficult memory: Essays on the Jewish genocide], 157–97. Athens: Vivliopolion tis Estias, 2012.

Yacoel, Yomtov. *Apomnimoneumata 1941–1943* [Memoirs 1941–1943]. Thessaloniki: Paratiritis, 1993.

Index

"Abbandono" movie, 43
"Eternal Melodies" movie, 31
"Final Solution", xxxi
"Iron crown" movie, 38
"Meltemi" camping, 81
"Viennesse Blood", 45

Abravanel, Moses, 45
Agency for the Custody of Jewish Property (YDIP), xix, xxxiv
Albania, 22
Alevi, Raphael, 66, 73n134
Alliance Israélite Universelle, xxxiv, 3
Amalias Street, xl, 57, 63, 64
Angel, Lucie, 89, 106n24
Antisemitic measures, xiii–xx, xxv–xxxi, xxxviii–xlv
Apollo (movie theater), 38
Argentina, xii, 60, 63, 64, 73n3, 73n5, 73n29
Askirou Mr., 72
Assael, Michel, 18, 51n4
Asseo, Henri, 106n29
Attias, Mr., 20
Auschwitz, xix, xx, xxv, xxvi, xxxii, xli, xlii, 3, 8, 81
Avayou family, 88, 93, 99, 102

Bar mitzvah, xxxvii, 15, 45
Barcelona, 60
Barouh - Covo, Lily, 60, 63, 64, 67, 69, 72
Barouh, Fredy (Alfred), xiii, xxvi, xxviii, 57–60
  Exchange of letters with his mother, 63–73
Barouh, Mathilde, xii–iii, xvii, xxvi, xxviii, xxv, xxxviii, 57, 58, 60–1
  Exchange of letters with her son, 63–73
Barouh, Yola, 57
Benaroya, Avraam, 90, 106n32
Benveniste, Daniel, 35, 46
Beth Saul Synagogue, 103, 107n60
Bialik, Haim, 46
Boutaris, Yannis, xi, xiv–v
BP Oil Company, 81
British Army, 81–2
Brunner, Alois, xxxi
Bulgaria, 79
  government, vxi
  occupation, xvi, xxvii
  atrocities, 82

Calderon, Annette, 57, 64–72
Calderon, Djiko, 64, 67–8, 71
Calderon, Henri, 63–8, 69–72
Cavalla, *see Kavala*
Cazes-Epitropou, Fani, 79, 81–3
Cazes, Albertos, xxvi, xxxv, 77–84
  Exchange of letters with his mother, 85–105
Cazes, Binouta, 79
Cazes, Marie, xiii, xv, xxviii, 80
Cazes, Mery, 106n40, 107n58

Cazes, Mathilde, 79
  Exchange of letters with her sons, 85–105
Cazes, Maurice, xiii, xxvi, xxxv, 77–84
  Exchange of letters with his mother, 85–105
Cazes, Menachem, 79, 106n40, 107n58
Cazes, Michel, xxx
Cazes, Neama, xii–iii, xvii, xxvi, xxviii, xxxv, xxxviii, 77–84
  Exchange of letters with her sons, 85–105
Cazes, Palomba, 79
Cazes, Samuel, 77
Cazes, Yehuda, 77, 107
Chatzimihail, Eleni, 77, 79, 83
Chatzimihail, Nikolaos, 82
Civilian Guard at the Ghetto, xxxv, l, 50, 103
Cohen, Leon, xxxvii
Communal Commission, xlix
Cosmidis, 31, 33, 37
Covo, Daniele, xii–xv, 58–60, 73
Covo, Ginette Stella, 60, 64, 72
Covo, Henri, 63–8, 70–2, 73n1

De la Salle School, 6
Deligiorgi Street, xl, 90
Deportations, xxvi, xxx, xl, xli–xliv, 48, 50
Didymoteicho (Demoticon), 30, 52n44
Djivre, Albert, 20, 30, 51n14, 53n68
Djivre, Avraam, 77
Djivre, Cloui, 46
Djivre, Eliezer, 30
Djivre, Mazaltov, 77
Drasi, *12*

EAM-ELAS, 81, 83n2
Eastern Rumelia, 79
Edmond Rostand Street, 99
Egypt, 8
Eichmann, Adolf, xivn13, xxxi
Ellinikos Voras, 12
Elytis, Odysseas, 82
Epitropou family, 79, 82

Fais, Moise, 27, 31, 52n35
Faltsi, Ourania, 20–1, 23, 26, 28, 40, 46, 51n2
Faltsis, Sotiris, xiii, xxxviii, 6, 8, 9, 15, 19–25, 32–6, 38–46, 51n10–11, 52n52, 53n72
Famine *see hunger*
Fatouros, Dimitris, 12
Fire of 1917, xliii
Floca pastry shop, 20, 51n13
Forced labor, xviii, xix, xxxi, xxxix, 51n14, 51n15

Gattegno, Albert, 90–1, 106n29, 40, 107n58
Geneva, 51, 63
Georgiou Nikolaidou street, 57
Ghettos, xix, xxii, xxvi–ii, xxix, xxxi–iii, xxxvii–iii, 3, 8, 57, 77, 106n44
  Baron Hirsch ghetto/transit camp, xxvi, xxxii–iii, xlix, 50, 67
  Living conditions, xxix, xv, xxxix, xl–i, 47
  Escape and deportation from ghetto, xli–iii
Gourgoulas, Costas, 30, 43
Gouzios, Kleantos, 86, 90, 101
Greco-Italian War, 79
Greek Army, 57, 79
Greek Mountaineering Club, 81
Greek Tour Club, 81

Haim, Bertica (Bertha), 31–2, 39, 43
Haim, Mr., 46
Hirsch hospital, 90
Hunger, xxxvi, xl, 39, 97

Integration of Thessaloniki 1912, xxxv
International Red Cross xxxvi, 51, 63
Ionos Dragoumi street, 6
Istanbul, 51n10, 57
Italias street, 86
Italy
  capitulation, 57, 81
  censorship, xxviii
  Italian consulate/consul, xlii, 96–7, 106n49
  school, 43
  soldiers, 8, 15, 38
  zone of occupation, xxvii, 8

Jani (Janaki), *see Triantafillidis Giannis*
Janitsa, 30, 42
Janni Drossopoulou Patission street, 94
Jewish cemetery of Thessaloniki, xviii, xxx, xxxix
Jewish Community of Athens, xvi

Jewish Community of Thessaloniki, xiii, xiv, xx, xxv, xxvii, xxx, xxiv–vi, xxxix, 1, 53n61, 77
Jewish Museum of Greece, xii, xvi, 57, 61, 77, 79, 82–4
Jewish Museum of Thessaloniki, xii, xxxiii, xxxvi, l

Kallithea, 79, 82
Kalogirou, Katina, 8, 23, 26, 30, 33, 51n10
Karaiscakis Street, 27
Karamihail, Menelaos, 100
Karapiperis, Doctor, 44–6
Kavala, 94, 106n42
Komotini, 79
Korai street, 20
Koretz, Sevy, xlvin35, xlix
Korytsa, 79

Larissa, 8, 15
Levy, Margot, 103, 107n61
Liberation, 81–83
Liberty square, xviii, xxx, xxxi, xxxix, 15
Lycée français, 21, 79
Lyon, 60

Makedonia, 12
Marcos, Irene, 17, 22, 25, 31, 34, 37, 40, 51n1
Miaoulis street, 100
Middle East Forces of the Allies, 57, 81–2
Misrahi street, 51n14, 90
Modiano Pastry Shop, 44
Modiano, Joseph, 94, 106n41
Molho, Joseph, 95
Molho, Maurice, 37
Molho, Michael, xxv, xlvn13

Naar, Beni, 45, 53n65
Naar, Esther, 42
Nahmias, Elda, 94
Nahmias, Isaac, 106n40
Nahmias, Marcos, 42
Nehama, Joseph, xxv, xliii
Neochori of Halkidiki 6, 15
Nicolaou, Nico, 20
Nissim, Gracien, 24

Ouziel, Ninette, 19, 34–5, 37, 42–3, 46, 51n9

Palaion Patron Germanou street, 6
Palanghias, Nico, 105
Papamoschou, Vassilis, 6, 8, 15, 20, 29, 33, 40, 45
Papas, Doctor, 36
Parente, Pepo, 64, 68, 70–1, 73n24
Paris, xii, xviii, 60, 82–3, 87
Pavlos Melas street, 22
Pelion, 81
Perahia, Germaine, xxxvii, 41, 53n61
Perahia, Jessua, xxxvii
Petroutsopoulos, Pendelis, 28–9, 33–4
Poland, xxxii, xli, xlii, 50
Politofilakas, see civilian guard at the ghetto
Prefecture of Magnisia, 82
Ptolemeon street xl, 46

Rafina, 81
Rezi Vardar, xix
Rimini, 57
Romanian Oil Company Steaua, 79

Salem, David, 106n40
Salem, Lisa, 93–4, 106n40
Saltiel (Nikolaou), Eleni, xii–iii, xv, 8, 14, 16
  Introduction by, 3–9
  Biography of Maurice Saltiel by 11–2
Saltiel, Isaak, 5–8, 11
Saltiel, Maurice, xiii, xvi, xxxviii, 3–9
  Autobiography excerpts, 13–5
  Exchange of letters with his mother, 17–51
  "Maurice Saltiel Hall", xiv
  Short biography, 11–12
Saltiel, Samy (Samico), 18–9, 23–4, 26, 28, 30–7, 39, 52n27
Saltiel, Sarina, xxvi, 3–9, 14–6, 51n5
  Exchange of letters with her son, 17–51
Schönberg, Fritz, xxxii
School of Fine and Applied Arts, 11
Second Boys High School, 6, 9
Segouras, 18–9, 23, 28, 31, 35, 37, 40, 46
Serrero, David, 3
Serrero, Gracia, 3
Serrero, Zak (Jacques), 18, 22, 28, 33, 36, 38–41, 44–5, 50–51, 51n5
Sissition (daily food allowance), xxxv
Solomon street, 44
Soulam, David, xxx

State Conservatory of Thessaloniki, 11, 51n4
State Orchestra of Thessaloniki, 11
State Theater of Northern Greece, 11
Stavroulakis, Nikolaos, xii, 77, 79
Sunday Vima, 79

Tiano, David, 90, 100
Titania (cinema theater), 39
Touring Club of Greece, 81
Triantafyllidis, Giannis, 8–9, 20–2, 24, 27–31, 33–38, 40–2, 45–6
Tsitsis, Diomidis, 23

United Front Party, xxx
University of Athens, xiv, 6
  Thinking of admission, 46
University of Macedonia, xii, xiv
University of Padua, 43
University of Thessaloniki, xiv, 82
Uziel, Jacques, 60, 67, 69

Valagianni School, 6
Vardaris, 6
Varsano, Salvator, 39, 41, 45, 53n58
Vasilissis Olgas – Analipisi, 79
Venizelos street, 6
Vilara street, 6
Volos, 57

Wisliceny, Dieter, xxxi

Yacoel, Yomtov, xxv

www.ingramcontent.com/pod-product-compliance
Lightning Source LLC
Chambersburg PA
CBHW061216210726
48294CB00006B/1861

9781805391340